THE PROCESS OF TRANSITION

1/31/23 Dear Son, I believe this
book is timely for the season you
are in. You are starting over.
transitioning into a new point
of your life. Read it and allow
it to help you in your transition
I love you.

Mom.

FYI - this is Pastor J.'s Book

THE PROCESS OF TRANSITION

REFORMING THE HEART FOR GROWTH

TAVARES D. ROBINSON

Watchman
PUBLISHING

Published by Watchman Publishing
www.watchmanpublishing.com
1-800-714-3194

Watchman Publishing is a Christian publisher that seeks to edify the local church by equipping individuals. We provide resources to admonish, exhort, reprove, and encourage the church in the Last Days.

Published and printed in the United States of America.

ISBN 978-1-7325134-4-0 (trade paper)

ISBN 978-1-7325134-5-7 (e-book)

Cover photography and design by Tanja Prokop

Editors: Leonard G. Goss and Carolyn Stanford Goss, GoodEditors.com, www.goodeditors.com

ACKNOWLEDGMENTS

I would like to thank Leonard Goss for his skillful editing of this manuscript.

I would like to thank Tonya Stampley and Jayda Hall for their tireless help in transcribing this message.

I would also like to thank the countless individuals who pushed me over the last few years to turn this teaching series into a book. Thank you for your encouragement.

And lastly, I would like to thank my Lord and Savior for revealing to me and trusting me to rediscover a priceless truth that has been buried. May your classroom of suffering once again be embraced by your people.

CONTENTS

PREFACE

As you peruse the landscape of Christendom, you will find an abundant amount of self-help books that have crept in stealthily to promise believers success if they follow a few steps. What these sorts of books share in common is quite disturbing: they eliminate the idea or concept of suffering. In today's church culture, the view of suffering and losing has been labeled as something that's negative or not Christlike; therefore, many of these books aim to "coach" you how to live in your "Promised Land," but they fail to teach you how to embrace your wilderness season.

Our Lord and Savior taught men how to die so they could live. Today's leaders are teaching men how to live; therefore, many despise the death process or are simply clueless to such requirement. For this reason, I am compelled to reintroduce to God's people his mandatory classroom for spiritual growth: the wilderness.

The apostle Paul declared, "I have been crucified with Christ and I no longer live, but Christ lives in me" (Gal. 2:20). This declaration should be the template for every follower of

Christ. But unfortunately, this statement does not become a reality in one's life because he or she verbally confesses it; there must come a time in our lives when God allows severe crucibles to transform our old nature into the new life, a renewed life.

I have written, *The Process of Transition: Reforming the Heart for Growth*, to guide end-time believers through the difficult, heart-wrenching, and challenging, yet rewarding process of being transformed into the image of Christ. If Paul had to endure three years in the desert, where he lost his image and abandoned his reputation to find Christ, then we must "Arm ourselves likewise," according to the words of the apostle Peter. God allows difficulties in our lives not to destroy us but to deepen us. Shallow Christianity only appeals to those who are driven by image branding, trendiness, and carnality. Don't be misled! In these Last Days, Christ is more concerned about our roots than our appearance.

I have learned over the years of walking with Christ that the life of a believer is filled with continued sacrifice— exchanging something of value for something that is of a greater value. As the saying goes, "Sometimes we have to lose something precious in order to gain something priceless." In our case, Christ is the prize and heaven is the reward.

INTRODUCTION

Transition—a term that has evolved into a popular buzzword in our day—has been greatly misunderstood. Some equate transition with change, but the two words do not have the same meaning. In most cases, God will initiate a change in order to bring forth a transition. Change usually happens instantaneously, while transition takes place over time. Change often entails a newness in external circumstances, while transition implies an internal transformation. Change is sudden, while transition is a difficult and daunting process that is governed by time.

We see these two words played out in the children of Israel's journey from Egypt into the wilderness. Their story is a great teaching tool for us on what to do and on what not to do. Admonishing the church at Corinth, Paul said, "These things happened to them as examples and were written down as warnings for us, on whom the culmination of the ages has come" (1 Cor. 10:11). According to Paul, God has preserved the historical story of the journey of his people for two reasons:

1) It is an example for us. Even though the children of Israel's encounters are long passed, they still remain as effective templates for our present and our future. If you take the time to study the lives of the children of Israel, you'll learn of how much their behaviors continue in ours. Neither the challenges they faced, nor the decisions they made will differ from our own. Let's not forget their destructive disobedience, which unfortunately, is just like ours too. Paul warned us of the danger of allowing pride to take hold of our lives simply because we have been privileged with salvation in Christ Jesus. "Our fathers" were also privileged but failed; in essence, they are us, and if we are not mindful, we will become like them.

2) It's meant to instruct us. In the Greek, the word for instruction or admonition is *nouthesia*. It means to influence one's mind by conveying what is right in order to avoid and prevent the wrong course of action. Paul was imparting a warning that their conduct and its consequences serve as a strong reminder not to repeat their mistakes.

The lives—good and bad—of those whom God exiled out of Egypt on the way to the Promised Land reveal the greatness of a beginning and the sorrow of an ending. They detail the wonderful and long-awaited change only to show the exiled people's hostile and unbending wills during transition. In essence, they were a people who initially celebrated but later regretted their change.

Let's gain a clearer understanding of the difficult and demanding challenges of transition by taking a macro-view starting at the origins of the history of the children of Israel. In Genesis chapter 12, God speaks to Abram about leaving his country and family to travel to a place that he will show him:

> The Lord had said to Abram, "Go from your country, your people and your father's household to the land I will show you. "I will make you into a great nation, and I will bless you; I will make your name great, and you will be a blessing. I will bless those who bless you, and whoever curses you I will curse; and all peoples on earth will be blessed through you" (vv. 1–3).

So Abram leaves and he eventually arrives at the place that God has appointed for him:

> Abram traveled through the land as far as the site of the great tree of Moreh at Shechem. At that time the Canaanites were in the land. The Lord appeared to Abram and said, "To your offspring I will give this land." So he built an altar there to the Lord, who had appeared to him. From there he went on toward the hills east of Bethel and pitched his tent, with Bethel on the west and Ai on the east. There he built an altar to the Lord and called on the name of the Lord" (vv. 6–8).

As time progresses, God visits Abram again and this time speaks concerning the prophetic destiny of Abram's descendants:

> Then the Lord said to him, "Know for certain that for four hundred years your descendants will be strangers in a country not their own and that they will be enslaved and mistreated there. But I will punish the nation they serve as slaves, and

afterward they will come out with great possessions. You, however, will go to your ancestors in peace and be buried at a good old age" (Gen. 15:13–15).

God never hid from Abram what his descendants would have to face. They would have to endure difficult times, but in the end, God would bring them out. The same applies to us as New Testament believers—neither Jesus nor his apostles ever hid what we must endure:

 If anyone comes to me and does not hate father and mother, wife and children, brothers and sisters—yes, even their own life—such a person cannot be my disciple. And whoever does not carry their cross and follow me cannot be my disciple" (Luke 14:26–27).

Christ is, indeed, loving and merciful, but he is not concealing the demands and cost of being a true follower. The Lord once again reminds us of the trouble we will have to face: "I have told you these things, so that in me you may have peace. In this world, you will have trouble. But take heart! I have overcome the world" (John 16:33). Paul tells us, "In fact, everyone who wants to live a godly life in Christ Jesus will be persecuted" (2 Tim. 3:12). Finally, Peter's first epistle says, "To this you were called, because Christ suffered for you, leaving you an example, that you should follow in his steps" (1 Pet. 2:21). As God has informed us of the hardship of this life while following his Son, he also reminds us that he had earlier informed Abram of his descendants' trouble.

The trouble would commence after God raises up Joseph.

Out of spite and envy, his brothers sell him into slavery to a nomadic tribe who takes him to Egypt, where he becomes a slave to Potiphar, an appointed officer of Pharaoh and a captain of the guard.

Sometime later, God fulfills the promise he had spoken to Joseph (Gen. 37:5–11), and Joseph is now second in power over all of Egypt (Gen. 41:1–57). Joseph eventually reveals to his brothers who he is, and Jacob and the entire family move from the Land of Promise to Egypt (Gen. 46:1–34). After Jacob dies, Joseph's brothers are troubled that he will take revenge upon them, but Joseph reveals that God has sent him to preserve their posterity, and they will live in Egypt in peace (Gen. 50:19–26).

Joseph dies, centuries pass, and another Pharaoh ascends who does not know of Joseph. At this time, the numbers of the children of Israel grew so rapidly, the biblical account says the "land was filled with them" (Exod. 1:7). The new Pharaoh then devises a plan to afflict them and make their lives bitter with bondage (Exod. 1:8–14) so their numbers will not grow as quickly.

The plan does not succeed. In fact, it actually causes the children's numbers to increase, which led Pharaoh to hatch another plan: kill all the newborn boys. In this decision, we see the attributes of God in operation:

- His providence: his ability to govern all our circumstances by directing situations to his desired ending.
- His sovereignty: his ability to have control in any circumstance; therefore, he is free from any outside controlling influences.
- His goodness and perfection of character: he will

do what is in our best interest in harmony with his divine will.

Even though time passed by, God never lost sight of his promise to Abraham. And knowing that time was approaching for their exodus, he allowed affliction and hardship to arise.

Like us, the children of Israel became comfortable in a place that was designed to be temporary, so God allowed pain. They outgrew their temporary location, and it became a place of bondage. Similarly, when we stay in a place longer than we should, it will no longer bring us contentment. It will now become a place of dread that fuels internal turmoil. When we reach this place, God is initiating change.

Throughout the book of Isaiah, God constantly reminds us of his influence in jumpstarting change:

- "I am the Lord; that is my name! I will not yield my glory to another or my praise to idols. See, the former things have taken place, and new things I declare; before they spring into being I announce them to you" (42:8–9).
- "Forget the former things; do not dwell on the past. See, I am doing a new thing! Now it springs up; do you not perceive it? I am making a way in the wilderness and streams in the wasteland" (43:18–19).
- "I foretold the former things long ago, my mouth announced them and I made them known; then suddenly I acted, and they came to pass" (48:3).

God is not shy or reserved about his power or acts. Because he is God, pride will never be his struggle or downfall. He is never embarrassed by his foreknowledge or omniscience; therefore, he does not shirk away from proving and declaring that he alone is the first and only one who can speak and initiate change.

Perusing the Scriptures, we will see that every change or transition was originated by God's prophetic decrees. Men who believe they can speak and change times and seasons based on their perceived "spiritual authority" are self-deluded, prideful, and self-deceived. God changes circumstances by his will, for his purpose, and not by humans' personal ambitions.

Looking again at how God spoke to Abraham, we see God had earlier revealed to him his ultimate plan for the Jewish people: captivity in a foreign land; deliverance from that land; and a return back to the Land of Promise. God governed all of these events in his timing. The prophet Daniel later spoke concerning God's influence over time: "Praise be to the name of God for ever and ever; wisdom and power are his. He changes times and seasons; he deposes kings and raises up others. He gives wisdom to the wise and knowledge to the discerning" (Dan. 2:20–21). God governs time by his Word, and not by our needs, expectations, or wants.

When God was ready to change the times concerning his people's slavery in Egypt, he sent a word—and it was sent through Moses. Moses' declaration to Pharaoh was the vehicle that set in motion the Israelites' transition (Exod. 5:1). Their experiences illustrate the difference between change and transition. He brought them out of Egypt quickly (change) with a desire to transform their character in the wilderness (transition). God can change our external circumstances swiftly, but it is the internal reforming that is a process.

Noting that many today have developed an unhealthy appetite for unsound and flesh-appealing teachings (2 Tim.

4:1–4), I propose to explain the difficulty and pain of walking with God and to reintroduce believers back to his training ground, our wilderness. Many books have been written on the subject of transition, and I do not claim to be an original thinker or an expert on this subject, but I do have personal experiences with transition. My experiences have led me to an increasing understanding that compels me to write this book.

In 2012, while making preparations to leave my home for the day, I heard the word *transition* echo loud within me. The sound was so convincing I stopped and pondered on what I had just heard. After a short period of silence, I realized the Lord was getting my attention to seek him. This encounter resulted in the Holy Spirit teaching me his process of transition, which I later taught at my church, not realizing that within a year my life would take an unexpected turn—transition would be knocking on my door.

The book you are now reading is the product of that series. I believe it is God's timing for me to share this message. Therefore, I desire to help others safely navigate the rugged and heart-wrenching terrain of transition. Many wish for butterfly endings but loathe caterpillar alterations. It is for this reason I have written *The Process of Transition: Reforming the Heart for Growth.*

Every stage of transition God appoints, he designs to conform our hearts to his will for a particular purpose. The root word for "reform" in Greek is *diorthosis.* It means to amend, to correct, or to straighten something that has moved away from its original condition. In other words, it means to accomplish a complete rectification when that which is inadequate and imperfect gives place to that which is productive and perfect.

When God desires to conform your heart, he is not

referring to our physical body part. The heart he is denoting is known as *kardia* in the Greek; it is a picture of what controls a person's personality, motives, desires, decisions, choices, thoughts, emotions, and will. It's the internal "command center" that is responsible for producing the correct output to life's challenging demands. In essence, a reformed heart is when the mind, desire, and will have been corrected and straightened back to their original positions in order for the heart to respond correctly to the will of God. When one's heart correctly aligns with God's will, transformation and growth will take place.

I'll never forget the conversation I had with my next-door neighbor who is a pilot for a major airline company in America. As we discussed the temperament of some of the passengers he encounters during flight times, he said, "For us pilots, it's all about the journey, but for passengers, it's all about the destination."

This is true, and our hurry to reach our destination can also apply to our relationship with God. Many times, we are impatient and at odds with him. He is a God of patience who takes delight in our learning from each step of the journey; we are, in contrast, inherently impatient and only look forward to the end result. But transition is indeed a process. It will, at times, seem undesirable, but it is necessary. There will be moments of unexplained pain, but the pain is purposeful. It will always come at an unexpected time because God controls the time. Contrary to how it feels, it is really an expression of his love. Contrary to how it looks, it is really God's launching pad into his promise.

There will be moments when you feel like complaining. Don't do it. Instead, learn how to be thankful. There will be moments when you feel as if God has forsaken you. Be patient. He is testing you. When transition is underway, class is in session. God is teaching you who he is and who you are not. It is humbling, shameful, and at times embarrassing, but we must remember: a servant is not above his master (Matt. 10:24). If Christ is our Lord, let us arm ourselves likewise.

In Egypt, God meets us with his salvation; in the wilderness, we meet God for our maturation. Paul explains our condition:

 But we have this treasure in jars of clay to show that this all-surpassing power is from God and not from us. We are hard pressed on every side, but not crushed; perplexed, but not in despair; persecuted, but not abandoned; struck down, but not destroyed. Through suffering, our bodies continue to share in the death of Jesus so that the life of Jesus may be visible in our bodies, even though we live under constant danger of death. Because we serve Jesus, we face physical death, but his death has resulted in eternal life for us. We continue to preach because we have the same kind of faith the psalmist had when he said, "I believed in God, so I spoke." We know that God, who raised the Lord Jesus, will also raise us with Jesus and present us to himself. All of this is for our benefit. And as God's grace reaches more and more people, there will be great thanksgiving, and God will receive more and more glory. His grace and hope are why we never give up. Though our bodies are dying, our spirits are being renewed every day. Our present troubles are small and won't last very long. Yet they produce for us a glory that vastly outweighs them and will last forever! Don't look at the troubles you can see now; rather, fix your gaze on things that cannot be seen. For the things we see now will soon be gone, but the things we cannot see will last forever" (2 Cor. 4:7–18).

PART ONE

DETACHMENT

$\mathcal{W}$e live in a spiritual era where some spiritual leaders elevate the significance of the promises we receive after transitioning as higher than the actual transition process itself. Pastors boast in the fact that "God is going to transition you into something that will blow your mind!" And while this statement holds weight, there are several hidden truths that must be revealed for the sake of our faith. First, true transition is not self-initiated. Every true transition begins and ends with God. Secondly, the transition that God takes you through will cost you everything—a truth that many leaders fail to mention to believers. We have fallen for this idea that pain we feel from traumatic life experiences sets us up only for this great promise from God. We believe that we won't have to worry about growing into spiritually mature people because God counted that pain as enough for a promise. The fact that we went through hurt is enough, we say to ourselves, forgetting that we must respond correctly in order to receive whatever God has for us. It is as if we have grown to believe a new thing will come to pass in our lives for free.

Before we dive into what I consider to be four steps of transition that God takes believers through, it is important that we debunk the half-truths we have believed. You can be sure that God cares about the details of our lives—yes, he is concerned and is always watching over us, even during times of trouble. Nevertheless, we cannot compare God to one of those teachers who stumbled into the field because other career paths didn't work out. God is not in the business of simply passing us on our terms or because he wants us to like him.

It is true that God can allow your bad decisions and past mistakes to work for your good, especially if those decisions led you straight to him. But now something significant has to happen to move you into God's will for your life. How does God get you out of your wrong decision? How does he remove you from a situation where you've invested so much time? How does God correct your faulty thinking even though you believe you are right? How does he relocate you from a place you put yourself? He does it with transition, and a painful one at that.

You may say to yourself, "Well, I've been through pain before, so I'm sure whatever God puts me through will be just like any other time." If this is a monologue you are repeating in your mind, stop right there. Do not be deceived. God has a way of shaking up our lives with circumstances we won't see coming—ask Job (Job 3:1–26). But this is where God tests our trust in him. Can you trust God to see you through the process as much as you trust him to fulfill his promise?

When God decides to spark this change in our lives, we

can be sure that the heartbreak we experience will be on him. King Solomon declared that there is a season for every event under heaven (Eccles. 3:1–8). The time of heartbreak is a particular season where we feel every sting that will pierce our hearts deeply. It is a time where we cannot dare to point the finger at Satan as if he is the object of our pain. In fact, God does not want us pointing fingers at anyone; he wants the heartbreak to shift our focus onto him. This unwavering concentration on God is necessary to pass each stage and to overcome every obstacle that seeks to disqualify us.

So how does God assist us in our transitioning? He will walk us through four particular stages that are not for the faint of heart: detachment, disidentification, disappointment, and disconcertment. Before God walks us through these stages, he allows us to hear his Word, and if we receive it, our faith will have enough flame to move us to the first step, as Jesus prayed it would for his disciple Simon (Luke 22:32). So the flip side must be that if God does not speak, we cannot move.

Sadly, Scripture context has been the least of worries for many believers, making it difficult for them to recognize if God is even speaking directly to their hearts. But it's important for a believer preparing to walk through these four stages to hold on to the Word of God and its context. King David, when faced with a very challenging season, said: "Remember your word to your servant, for you have given me hope. My comfort in my suffering is this: Your promise preserves my life" (Ps. 119:49–50). Walking a journey with God and having no idea of what his Word means will set one up to be stuck in a season that the Lord never prepared him or her for. Do you know the meaning behind the phrase "new season?" This popular catch phrase has circulated throughout church history for years and continues to blow itself into the mouths of many who are tired of the season they are currently in. But just because we have had enough of our circumstances does not mean God is ready to move us along. God always initiates change for himself and not because we are tired.

CONFRONTATION FROM THE WORD

*I*f God had no intentions of transitioning you, he would have never allowed you to hear the message you heard. Sometimes you may wonder how is it that a sermon was tailored just for you. You might ask yourself, "Did someone tell the pastor about me? Are my issues that obvious?" As the Word came forth for the entire congregation, it seemed as if the spotlight beamed on you. The writer in the book of Hebrews mentions how potent the Word of God is when spoken under the influence of the Holy Spirit: "For the word of God is alive and active. Sharper than any double-edged sword, it penetrates even to dividing soul and spirit, joints and marrow; it judges the thoughts and attitudes of the heart" (4:12).

When the Word confronts us in this way, we must recognize that this is a point of transition where God desires to start a new journey in our lives. However, if we try to initiate this change on our own, it will always end in failure.

GOD'S TIMING AND OUR RESPONSIBILITY

*T*here will always be a moment in which God brings us to a point of knowing his will, but there is *one* problem. Many people receive this knowledge and reject it because it does not meet their expectations. Countless struggle to hear the voice of the Lord because they have already determined, within themselves, what he would not speak. But one truth I have grown to learn is that the will of God will always run contrary to our expectations or felt needs. If we are not careful, we can be so driven by our expectations that when they don't come to pass, we struggle mentally to overcome. Imagine this: If Christ would have met the demands of people who pressed him, he would have died as an old man and never been crucified. If you haven't noticed, God brings us into what he wants for our lives and not what we think is a good idea. He accomplishes this change in our lives at an accurate and perfect time. This attribute is what makes God who he is. Could you imagine a God who is always late when it's time to deliver you or transition you? Your life would lie in ruins because God would have had no idea how to master time. Take note of this: if God shows up late one time, he will cease to be God.

Thanks be to God that his timing is not our issue. We have a responsibility to trust God because his character is without fault (Deut. 32:4). For this reason, we shouldn't expect him to show up at a time we deem appropriate. How many times did you want God to show up for you in the last year and he didn't? You thought your situation was bad then, and when he didn't appear, you didn't know how you were going to make it. Fast forward to today, God either showed up at the perfect time or still has you waiting, which shows how much you've grown to depend and lean on him. Everything about God is right; everything he does is right; everything he allows is right.

Trusting God and his ways is just part of our responsibility. A belief has been floating around in the modern-day church that suggests, "If it is God's will, it will just happen." If you have grounded your life on this faulty belief, let me be the first to tell you this is not entirely true. In God's will, there is his ultimate decree, or what we call *will*. Following that will is his heart's intention or desire. We've read in Scripture things that transpired as a result of God's decree. These moments will continue to take place because God said it and he cannot lie. But 1 Timothy 2:4 also reads, God "wants all people to be saved and to come to a knowledge of the truth."

If you look around, many people are falling away from believing in God and in Jesus' death on the cross and leaning more to "positive and negative energies." While God desires for all to come to him, the truth is that not everyone will. And it isn't because God hasn't made provision for salvation but when the opportunity comes to receive, strong-willed people reject it.

As for us as believers, God will do whatever he must so that we know "this is the moment." We must make sure we know God's will and that we are walking in it.

THE CHALLENGE

*W*hen God transitions us, challenges will arise to develop us, to remove distractions from us, and to close doors in our lives. God is basically rewiring, and he does this by influencing our external circumstances in order to get us to change. These circumstances will feel like death itself because we come to the realization that things we thought we knew, we really don't know. The challenges are so vigorous that we will question if we even know God. As a matter of fact, we will never truly learn God's will until he brings us to a place where we know nothing. This test brings us to a place where we realize although we have been believers for years, we are really infants in the eyes of God. Truth be told, we really don't understand what is going on.

It is at this moment when God brings us to a place of humility. Why? Because God will never start a new season in our lives prior to humbling us. Humility is always God's platform for promotion. Regardless of where we are in God or how far he intends to elevate us, God will always orchestrate a series of events in our lives for the intended purpose of humbling us. Humility is always the platform from which promotion comes. This is why Solomon, the wisest man to ever live, says, "Before a downfall the heart is haughty, but humility comes before honor" (Prov. 18:12). Promotion from God will never transpire as a result of one's pride.

A hindrance to growing in this challenge is thinking that we are not prideful at all. We believe we are humble because we respect everyone, we are soft spoken, we are willing to go last, and we stay out of people's way. We can have all of these traits and still be prideful persons in the sight of God. In fact, when God challenges our pride, we will realize how much humility we actually lack. *Humility* means "being brought low." Before God manifests a promise to each of us, he will allow us to fail in our own strength. He does this so we won't think we are naturally qualified for what he is about to do. He is not the author of sin, but he will allow us to fail in our own strength so when his will manifests, we won't attribute it to our qualifications or lack of them, but to God keeping his promise to us—ask Peter (Luke 22:31–34). When God brings the promise, we will understand that we were not deserving. Had he never allowed us to fail, we would think we were worthy of receiving his blessing. God will allow us to be at the bottom, so when he fulfills his promise, we will be confident in testifying, "I did not deserve it, God!"

Today, the church talks little about these challenges. We have learned how to be blessed without first being humbled, as if God will elevate us without touching undone areas in our lives. We have been taught Promised Land victories while neglecting wilderness crucifixions. If God does not confront the pride in us, we will have the tendency to use our power to control instead of lead, and to intimidate instead of serve. God has blessed us all with some kind of gift and ability, but he will never elevate our gifting above humility. We should never ask God to show us his will if we are not ready to forsake who we are. The beginning of Christ working in us will happen once we reach the end of ourselves.

DETACHMENT IS A COMING APART

$\mathcal{H}$ aving laid down some foundation, let us move into stage one of transition—detachment. The first two stages impact us physically and emotionally, while the last two stages impact us spiritually. *Detachment* in this discussion is the act of actually coming apart, a sort of separation, if you will. It is no longer being personally or emotionally involved with something. This stage is what keeps people from moving forward with God. When we are truly attached to something we have invested so much time and attention into, it is more than difficult to let go. Even if this thing causes us pain, we will hang on for dear life because this is where our comfort lies. We can get in the habit of being comfortable with something familiar, even though it is dysfunctional. We know it is dysfunctional but continue with it because we know how to function in it. We do not want to gamble with the unknown. God knows this. So he begins to allow certain things to transpire in the place where we are familiar. We start to feel as if we are losing. Everything begins to appear contrary. All odds seem to be against us, and we are failing in the place where we once had victory and security. Things are being shaken. And naturally, our prayer is, "God, keep it! Fix it! Put it back together!" But God's desire is to end it.

We want transition but we don't want to be detached from what we used to know. We don't want to cut loose some people, places, and things we have depended upon. It's tough! We want to keep permanent the things that God says are only temporary. We'll gladly sever relationships with those who have been of no benefit. It's hard, however, to cut loose those who once upon a time were a help to us. What we have to now realize is that some relationships were designed to take us only so far. Every affiliation isn't meant to be long-term.

When it comes to God's will or plan for us, we cannot always expect a nonstop flight. Sometimes, connecting flights are necessary because the first flight can only take you so far. It is foolish to stay on the plane when it has already reached its destination, but many will remain because they've become comfortable in their seats. We don't understand that this flight was only designed to take us to a certain hub where we will have to get off and find our way to the gate of our next flight. We will have to make the effort, but it's not as difficult as it seems because our ticket will tell us which gate we are to change to next.

God will not have us transition unless he has already given us information for the next gate. We just have to be willing to do some work. When we finally reach this gate, we must not become too comfortable with how God brought us to our current destination. He does not guarantee that we will be on a nice, quiet flight to the final destination. We may find ourselves on a noisy, compact and uncomfortable aircraft, but this small plane is necessary to get us to where we need to be.

Another struggle with detachment is when God begins to cut us from ourselves. "That's just who I am," we may say. Then God starts to cut us from the very person we say we are. Other times, we claim, "That isn't me." But God cuts again, and this time, it is from the very person we say we are not. He is coming after it all. We can eventually cut loose from the people who no longer belong in our lives. The real struggle will be cutting free from ourselves. It's hard to separate from self when we still find value in it. Martin Luther, theologian and reformer, said, "The person that I am most terrified of is not Satan. It is me!"

When life happens, we have a way of becoming shaped into something God never desired for our lives. Hurt, regret, rejection, and disappointment, all have had their share in shaping humankind. Always being overlooked or never being acknowledged have a way of changing us. Trying to earn the approval of people only to be rejected even more does something to the heart. In fact, those who receive the most rejection in their lives happen to love the hardest. So, when God walks them through detachment, it is hard for them to break their loyalty and disconnect. People will sit in a bad relationship, knowing the relationship is not fruitful, because they feel they've invested too much to leave. They are hoping God will revive it.

God will never revive anything he hasn't started. However, there will be a period where God gets each of us alone—ask Jacob (Gen. 32:24). For the first time in twenty years, Jacob was alone with God. This period of isolation was not about what Jacob could receive from God; it was about what God was determined to get out of Jacob. Some of us can display forms of showmanship in front of others, but who we are alone is the true measurement of our character. Jacob was willing to hold on while God uprooted self-dependency, self-reliance and craftiness. This showed Jacob's great desire to be broken. But people who suffer from rejection will struggle with handling this alone time. Rejection can stain and shape us and have us insisting, "This is who I am." That, however, is not who God wanted us to become. God will take us through this process to undo what life and hurt did to us. Additionally, if we are used to controlling our lives, it is offensive for someone to tell us to trust God. How do we take our hands off our disturbed lives when our sanity came from our hands being on it?

When God is detaching us from something, he is saying, "Don't miss your window." He puts us in a dilemma where we have to choose between obeying him or maintaining this reputation of loyalty. When God is detaching us, he will call us out of the commitments we may have pledged. This is a time we must prepare ourselves for the gossip that will spew out of the mouths of those who once knew us. This is part of the process of God breaking us, and others will not understand who we are becoming.

Will we defend ourselves? Or will we trust God's process? We should not defend ourselves regarding relationships God never told us to commit to in the first place. We must be able to hear God, despite what remaining silent may do to our reputation.

DETACHMENT IN SCRIPTURE

*D*etachment is not just a modern-day move that God recently started to initiate. It has been a stage that many, even in Scripture, had to undergo. God has detached people from their culture, from situations they have created, and even from their perceptions.

DETACHING US FROM WHAT WE HAVE KNOWN

God started the detachment process for Peter and his brother Andrew in Matthew 4:19–20, where he commands them to "'Come, follow me ... and I will make you fishers of men.' At once they left their nets and followed him." Jesus approaches Jewish men who have responsibilities and tells them in so many words to drop all they have known and follow behind him. In the Greek, the word for "drop" or "left" is *aphiēmi*. It means to divorce, to abandon, to go away and leave something behind. Jesus was telling these disciples to disconnect and disengage themselves when loyalty was all they knew. They had to be sure that Christ was the Messiah to forsake family in order to follow him. When God initiates transition, he is going to call us out of something that would bring us pain. He is closing a door that we thought would remain open. He will cut people loose who we thought would be riding with us forever. And all of that will require us to surrender our will and trust him.

Peter and Andrew weren't the only two who were detached from what they were so accustomed to. John and his brother James also had to experience the daunting task of detachment in Mark 1:19–20. The call to follow Christ demanded that they forsake their father and the fishing business, which was their source of income. Detachment shook the children of Israel, as well. This crowd could never fully transition with God because they struggled to let go of their past in Egypt. The Bible accounts describe how the children of Israel always wanted to go back to slavery whenever circumstances transpired that they weren't expecting (Exod. 16:3; 17:3; Num. 14:3). Detachment moved them to a place of having to trust God, something they didn't have to do in a controlled environment in Egypt. Yes, they were being beaten, and even treated unjustly, but the familiarity is all they knew and thus, the harsh treatment was easier to handle versus trusting God for what they could not see (Exod. 1:1–22; 5:1–23). They failed to realize that when someone is a slave to anything other than God's will, that person will be disqualified for the promise.

We see this truth in the life of Moses, the one called to deliver the children of Israel from Egypt. Forty years prior, Moses attempted to be Israel's deliverer in his own timing, through his own pride and ambitions, and failed (Exod. 2:11–15; Acts 7:17–36). Forty years later, God sent him back to the Israelites broken and humbled. Because of God's covenant with Israel, God did not allow the "son of Pharaoh" to deliver his people. Later, a shepherd—and a servant of God—would be their deliverer, but not without paying a great price.

God will arrange extreme testing in our lives to strip us from the identity of the world. His goal is to bring us into conformity with his will. For this reason, God designed the wilderness in order to get "Egypt" out of his people's minds and hearts. The children of Israel saw the Red Sea swallow up their enemies. How much more extreme could such an event be? Still, they longed to go back to how things used to be. They had witnessed firsthand how God transitioned them with a word sent through Moses.

"Let my people go!" Moses' order started the transition. It's only then that the process began. They praised God initially because he parted the Red Sea. Women praise danced with tambourines for the first time (Exod. 15:1–21). They trusted God because they saw him overthrow the riders. And then, just a few days later, they murmured and complained about a lack of water (Exod. 15:22–27). The children of Israel wanted to go back to the place where they ate melons and onions.

"Why did you bring us out here? Were there no graves in Egypt?" Their complaining began even before God opened up the Red Sea (Exod. 14:11–12), and sadly, they never grew beyond such conduct. Why? God had delivered them, but they were never disengaged from Egypt in their loyalties.

God works a miracle to bring each of us out physically, but our hearts may still be entangled. As long as our hearts are still entangled, Satan will use the entanglement to keep us in bondage. This was the dilemma with Lot's wife. God rescued her along with her family from his judgment, but she disobeyed the warning given because her heart longed more for her desire than for God's mercy (Gen. 19:12–26). The consequences of her action serve as a reminder for us today. Jesus prophetically warned, "Remember Lot's wife!" (Luke 17:32); the word *remember* is written in present imperative tense in the Greek. It means to continue to call to mind, to think of, and to make mention of. It recalls what Lot's wife was commanded to do and how she willingly chose to disobey.

Lot's wife serves as an example of a person who is so attached to the things of this world that it's hard to obey God's instructions. Every time we hear her name we should remember the dangerous consequences of loving this life over the life to come. When God cuts things, he severs them. This is where the heartbreak begins. God cuts us off from what we are familiar with and puts us in a place where we are vulnerable and trembling. It does not seem like something God would do, but that's right where he wants us. When we are vulnerable, fearful, unsure, and insecure, he wants us to turn to him.

DETACHING US FROM WHAT WE HAVE CREATED

Whatever God is going to do, he will wait until your belief dies. He will wait until all of your means and plans are exhausted and your expectation of how you think he will act proves to be false. God did the same thing with Abraham. He gave him a prophetic promise but did not allow it to manifest until Abraham exhausted all of his means and plans for how God should fulfill it. He waited until Abraham was one hundred years old and Sarah's womb was barren due to old age (Gen. 17:15–21).

The first time God spoke—when Sarah was seventy-five

years of age—she believed that she could still bear a child in her strength. We don't laugh at what God says when he first speaks because we believe our "womb" can do it. But when God allowed her womb to die and told Abraham again that he would fulfill his promise for Sarah to bear a child, Sarah laughed in disbelief (Gen. 18:1–15). She had believed him at first, at least until time began to set in and nothing happened. It was at that point that she got creative, putting into play her own plans (Gen. 16:1–16). God waited for her womb to die before manifesting his Word because no one would be able to get the glory but him.

God works the same way today. His plans are not our plans and his timing is not our timing. We cannot get up and testify about the amount of faith we had by claiming, "I just knew he would do it!" Truth is, for many of us, we didn't even believe at one point in time. It looked bleak for us at one moment and inwardly we started to struggle. The level of faith many believe they have is an idol. They have grown to have faith in their faith, which is erroneous. There is no way a person can "naturally" believe God for what he promised. God has to put something in us to believe him. It is not *our* faith. Jesus did not teach us to have faith in ourselves, but to have faith in God (Mark 11:22). He has to put *his* faith in us to believe him for something that will happen down the road. This is the time where the Devil will show us everything contrary to shake our faith. But faith in God is total dependency on him. It is the belief that he, who spoke the Word, is well able to perform it and do it. Faith pleases God because we are placing total dependency upon the person who spoke it.

Abraham's hope did not align to God's until Abraham's original hope died (Rom. 4:18). When Abraham got to the end of what he thought, then hope in God kicked in. As he did with Abraham, God will always bring us to the end of ourselves. As a matter of fact, he will not even get to the point of disciplining us until we come to the end of who we are. That is the first stage of discipleship—God has to bring us, both you and me, to the end of "you" and "me." All true discipleship is about losing and dying, not gaining and living.

To be taught any other view of discipleship is misleading. Christ taught about taking up our cross daily and following him. He taught the disciples how to die, but today we have men who pretend to be sent by Christ and teach many how to live for themselves. Receiving a certificate of completion from a discipleship class is not what God requires to approve your discipleship. The first lesson in discipleship is about losing—losing your life, losing your desires, losing yourself, losing your dreams, and losing your importance.

We will touch on this aspect of discipleship in the next stage of transition. Losing one's self is a lost truth that deserves to be discovered, especially in an age where many are determined to "find" themselves. If all we've learned in discipleship class was about church protocol, spiritual positions and titles, and gifts we can put to use for the Kingdom, then our foundation is already faulty.

May the Lord help us recover the true meaning of this truth, for our evangelism is only as accurate as our discipleship. Once God brings us to that point of forsaking ourselves, he will have the access to build us according to his will. Abraham had an Ishmael, but God has an Isaac in mind. Ishmael came as a result of Abraham and Sarah's creativity. But in order to get the promise, we are going to have to wait. It is easier to be creative ourselves than it is to wait on God's creativity because waiting will always require faith and patience.

DETACHING US FROM OUR PERCEPTIONS

Samuel was one of the greatest prophets in the Scriptures. God had used him mightily to prophesy to Israel when he was about to transition them. At this time, the nation was being ruled by judges and was about to move into kingship. God used Samuel to guide the people at this time. But even the prophet who heard God with such keenness and accuracy (1 Samuel 3:19) nearly made a mistake as God initiated transition; Samuel became dependent on what he saw rather than on what he had heard. When it was time to transition to God's appointed king, he went to Jesse's house in search of someone who looked a lot like King Saul.

A word of caution here: One of the worst things we can do is to follow a ministry that is patterning itself after other ministries that God has already rejected. If God is detaching you from your current church, don't assume the will of God will come in a package that looks familiar to your old church. Samuel was trying to determine the will of God by appearance. Samuel attempted to anoint David's older brother, Eliab, and God told him that Eliab was not the one. First Samuel 16:7 relates, "But the Lord said to Samuel, 'Do not look at his appearance or at his physical stature, because I have refused him. For the Lord does not see as man sees; for man looks at the outward appearance, but the Lord looks at the heart.'" In other words, God was saying that he promoted based on humility. God revealed to Samuel what he prized in his chosen king, and it did not match what Jesse thought God would prize; in the same way today, God never elevates one based on his or her appearance.

Imagine how humble David had to be to learn that he was chosen, although his father had not seen it fit to invite him to the lineup (vv. 8–13). The command was to "gather all your sons and prepare a banquet." David's brothers and Jesse just knew David could not be the chosen one based on his outward appearance. As a matter of fact, the Bible refers to David as "a young man" (1 Samuel 16:11; 17:33, 58). In Hebrew, the word "youngest" is *qatan*, which means one who is small, unimportant, and insignificant. The others were convinced that David could not be the one.

Samuel then asked Jesse if he had another son. Jesse had to have been shocked learning Samuel might be there to pick his youngest son, who was out in the field with the sheep. Who Jesse perceived should be king and who God knew should be king were two different sons. God knew the king he chose would need to be one who would tend to the people and one who had experience tending those who needed to be led. This king's platform would be built around feeding *God's sheep*, God's chosen people. God did not want someone similar to Saul, who would be recognized as king because of his status. God was looking for a king who understood that the first priority of a king was to obey God's command and be willing to put others' needs before his own.

Applying the account of God's anointing of David to our twenty-first century, we must quit trying to choose who or what God has already rejected. When God transitions us, the first thing we do is go out and pick up look-alikes. Once Samuel learned there was another son, he told Jesse to go get him, and then he anointed David to be king.

No one was about to get the credit or glory for what God

was about to do in David's life. God tells us what is to happen beforehand so that we know it is not because of our own strength or wisdom. He initiates the change, and before it springs forth, he is the one who tells you of it (Isa. 48:3–8).

Have you ever had moments where you just feel like enough is enough? Ever wonder how you can be involved in something for a long time and then out of the blue you become tired? This could be an indicator that God is initiating change. All of a sudden, you feel as if you can't take anything anymore. God has to get you to that point—otherwise, you will not transition. God leads you and puts in you the desire to seek him more. This is the pattern of God. He does not give you the whole picture, only a fragment. If he gave you everything, there would be no room for faith.

DETACHING US FROM THE CULTURE

This kind of detaching takes place because God is going to go against the grain and reveal to people who he truly is. God waited for Lazarus to die because he knew if he healed Lazarus, the people would think it was because of their prayers. God did not show up until the people's prayers ended, their power was exhausted, and they knew there was nothing else that could be done. God sent his Word through Jesus: "This sickness will not end in death. No, it is for God's glory so that God's Son may be glorified through it" (John 11:4). The truth was this: had Lazarus arisen before Jesus arrived, one or more persons could have stolen God's glory. So God did something that only God could do. He allowed Lazarus to die. His body lay until the time of natural decay (John 11:17). God knew the only way he would be glorified is if he moved in such a way that would resonate beyond the comprehension of those close to Lazarus. He allowed Lazarus's death to enter the stage where the people knew that nothing in their strength could resurrect their friend. They needed to realize that no level of strength, wisdom, or contingent planning could revive Lazarus.

Before Jesus called Lazarus to rise and come out of the tomb, God allowed him to be dead for four days; by this time, Lazarus's body would begin to stink. According to a Jewish traditional belief, once a man dies, his spirit hovers over the body for three days, as the death is not yet final. It is for this reason that it was custom for the Jewish people to pray over the dead for three days after death in hopes that perhaps the person would either be resurrected or make a peaceful transition into eternity. Jesus knew their belief, and as a result, waited four days, until the body began to stink and stiffen and the people believed Lazarus's spirit no longer hovered over him (John 11:38–45).

Think about it. Just one day after Lazarus died, the people would still have had hope in their ability to bring him back through prayer. Even after the second day, optimism would not have seemed strange. But by day four, the people's confidence in delivering Lazarus from his deathbed through prayer would have disappeared and they would have believed Lazarus's spirit had made it to its final resting place. The Jewish people knew with certainty that the window of resurrection had ended and it was impossible for Lazarus to rise. It was then that God, through Jesus, fulfilled the Word he sent, telling Lazarus, "Come forth!"

When you apply the account of how God detached Lazarus from the customary three-day waiting period to your life today, you will find that God may detach you from the way the culture operates. He will challenge the culture's way to show you that his way will always prevail.

DETACHING US FROM OUR WILL

In order to fulfill the will of his Father, Jesus had to go through a detachment stage. He had to leave heaven, giving up everything in eternity, to come down into time and submit himself to the rejection of the very people he had created. He had to, for the first time, experience his Father turn from him (Matt. 27:45–46). Jesus never had to experience that before coming to earth. It was to the point that while he bled profusely on the cross, he asked, "Why have you forsaken me?" He experienced rejection for the first time because his Father saw the sin of humanity.

This is a great prophetic picture of how Jesus suffered the forsaking of God so that we never have to experience it. But he had to first endure detachment. And he willingly became poor that we may become rich (2 Cor. 8:8–9). In other words, he gave up eternity and came into time so that we may have access to him. Contrary to devious Word of Faith or Prosperity Gospel teachings, these verses are not a reference to financial gain or material wealth. Paul uses this analogy: If Christ can give and sacrifice, why can't we? If Christ can sacrifice everything and subject himself to time, why can't we?

If we are ever to move into what God said, we will have to disengage. All four stages of detachment are tough, but this first one, letting go of our will, gets the ball rolling. It starts the process of our moving toward what God said. Even though it's part of our human nature to hold on to things that we are familiar with or love dearly, during this moment, we have to change how we pray. We will have to cease asking God to fix something that he is cutting out of our lives. To follow God, we first have to be detached. He will cause something to end without our input and without our permission. God often does this at an inconvenient time for us, allowing pain to manifest greatly. But as painful and as inconvenient as detachment may feel or be, we must not make the mistake to think detachment is not God's doing. Indeed, it is the start of transition manifesting in your life.

PART TWO

DISIDENTIFICATION

*T*ransition is a pleasant-enough word—until the process of transition starts. There is nothing pretty or pleasant about it; in fact, the only thing beautiful about transition is when it is over. This is a time when we must be ready to make a decision. We will either follow God's leading, or be lead by our own will—ask Orpah (Ruth 1:1–15).

All transitions begin with God ending something without our permission or input, and that ending moves us into detachment. Detachment occurs when God starts to cut things off and separates you from what you once knew. It is not limited to people, but can also include things within us. Detachment then leads to disidentification. This is where you begin to lose the person you have created. You start to lose the identity that people gave you. The disidentification stage eventually brings you to the place where you do not even know who you are in God. It leaves you wondering, *"Who am I, God?"* This is a painful place because it is the point where God has allowed things to happen for the purpose of "ruining" our image. While people hold on to reputation, God is looking at the image. Reputation is what people think you are. Your image is how God views you. Your reputation has no value with God, especially if it is contrary to the character he desires for you. The struggle is when you are trying to live according to the reputation others have put upon you. We are always trying to earn people's respect. When we do this, God considers our image illegitimate.

When your image is right with God, it does not matter how others view you. At the end of the day, you know you are in right standings with God. Jesus made himself of no reputation, submitting himself to God who judges righteously (Phil. 2:3–11). In other words, he did not have to continue to prove to people who he was as long as the Father was pleased. Anytime you are driven by reputation, you create an identity about yourself that God does not recognize as legitimate.

This was the attitude of the church in Sardis in the book of Revelation. God told them that they had a reputation of being alive, but to him they were really dead (Rev. 3:1). These people were more concerned with how others saw them than with God's view of them. Our greatest concern should be this: How does God see us? When we are sincere, God will show us how he views us. And we need to get ready for this moment because that revelation will be painful.

For this very reason, people reject transition. They don't want to face the truth that they weren't always who they believed they were. When God reveals the real us, he starts to show us things about ourselves that we did not know we still had in us. God brings us to a place where we will lose our identity so he can show us who he wants us to become. He shows us his image of each of us. After he does this, it should no longer matter what people think.

Before we can reach our destination in God, he's going to

have to get us to the point where the opinion of those around us will not drive us. He has to detox us so that he knows we will obey him despite how contrary it may be to the perception of others. It's only then we are qualified to fully obey God. Even getting to this place in God is a struggle for some, especially because we are living in a time where biblical love has been redefined. No one wants to come across as unloving. In fact, telling someone, "No" or simply disagreeing with someone for the sake of God's will often will find us labeled as "critical." No one wants to hear that they are negative or inconsiderate. So, oftentimes in an attempt to avoid these labels, we dodge the bullet of telling people the truth. But here is the truth: God's Word will offend even though our intentions are to be at peace with people. When the will of a man or woman is strong and has no intention to submit to the order of God, everything God has said or done will be offensive. There is no way around this.

In such situations, we must recognize the difference between conviction and condemnation. Condemnation occurs when people try to get you to live according to their standards. Conviction, on the other hand, is when the Spirit of God shows you, through the Scriptures, something that you are not. There is a difference.

Our image is what life has shaped each of us to become. And when we begin to walk through transition with God, he will take us through *disidentification*. He will take us through this moment where we start to lose who we thought we were. Disidentification is a struggle because we want to serve God but keep our image. We will learn that our strength, identity, and pride are connected to our image. He will put us in situations or troubles we don't think we deserve to be in because, after all, "I am his child, right?"

Galatians 2:20 is a transitional verse, one we must all walk through. We must agree with Paul:

> I have been crucified with Christ and I no longer live, but Christ lives in me. The life I now live in the body, I live by faith in the Son of God, who loved me and gave himself for me."

A crucifixion—not a physical one but a more important crucifixion of self—has taken place, Paul writes. And the byproduct of walking through that transition was the life that Paul then lived.

In Paul's words, we see what happens when God—not Satan, not other people, but God himself—ruins our image and who we think we are.

When God ruins our image, who can we run to? Nobody. We are now positioned to see ourselves. Once God ruins, we can't live by the reputation people have placed on us. In fact, when God ruins our image, people will still try to hold us to our reputation, causing an inner conflict to develop within us. People will esteem us, but we won't understand why they do because God has allowed us to see who we really are. We will reach a place where we know we cannot serve God holding onto that false image of ourselves.

God will ruin our image in front of everyone, taking everything we thought was private to expose it openly. People observing what is happening will think to themselves, "I thought that person had faith. I thought that person trusted God!" This is God ruining our image.

Disidentification is indeed a painful process for many, especially those whom God is calling out of churches that gave them a position and an identity. Although God is no longer there, such persons remain aboard sinking ships because their identities are tied to the positions the churches gave them. But the truth is, hearing God may lead us to a place where our image will not be esteemed. Other words or statements have masqueraded as ways to protect our image. People may say, "I have confidence in myself" or "I'm better than that" to cover up their attempt to ignore what's really an image protection issue. Paul wrote to believers about how God tears our images down because if anyone had an image, he did. Acts 23:6 says, "I am a Pharisee, descended from Pharisees." Paul's whole life had been devoted to being a highly esteemed Pharisee. Here, he gives background into his family and provides us with the long lineage of stock that he came from. He had a certain image, and his goal was to give us an idea of what it meant to give it all up. "I am crucified with Christ," he says. Philippians 3:4–11 describes Paul's self-image:

 If someone else thinks they have reasons to put confidence in the flesh, I have more: circumcised on the eighth day, of the people of Israel, of the tribe of Benjamin, a Hebrew of Hebrews; in regard to the law, a Pharisee; as for zeal, persecuting the church; as for righteousness based on the law, faultless. But whatever were gains to me I now consider loss for the sake of Christ. What is more, I consider everything a loss because of the surpassing worth of knowing Christ Jesus my Lord, for whose sake I have lost all things. I consider them garbage, that I may gain Christ and be found in him, not having a righteousness of my own that comes from the

law, but that which is through faith in Christ—
the righteousness that comes from God on the
basis of faith. I want to know Christ—yes, to
know the power of his resurrection and
participation in his sufferings, becoming like him
in his death, and so, somehow, attaining to the
resurrection from the dead."

Paul is pointing out that if anyone could have confidence
in their flesh, it should be him. He is saying that he, more than
anyone else, has the resume to have confidence in his own
ability. He begins to give a list. The first point is this: "On the
eighth day I was circumcised." Circumcision is important
because it is evidence of the covenant God made with
Abraham and reestablished with Moses (Gen. 17:9–14). If
anyone was a part of the covenant with God, they had to be
circumcised on the eighth day. It represented a relationship
with God. So, Paul tells us that his circumcision taking place
on the eighth day is evidence that he is the stock of Israel. He
is giving his lineage.

Paul continues: "[I am] of the tribe of Benjamin, a Hebrew
of Hebrews; in regard to the law, a Pharisee; as for zeal,
persecuting the church; as for righteousness based on the law,
faultless." Benjamin was one of the two favorite sons of
Jacob; the other was Joseph. Both Joseph and Benjamin were
sons through Rachel, the wife whom Jacob loved. This story
is interesting because when Benjamin, the younger of the two,
was born, his mother Rachel died (Gen. 35:16–19). At this
time, the nurse named him Ben-Oni, which means *son of my
sorrow*. But Jacob did not agree with this name. Instead, he
decided to call him "Benjamin," which means *son of my right
hand*. Benjamin was obviously loved by his father; therefore,

the Jewish people considered the tribe of Benjamin as especially favored. What Paul is letting us know is that he comes out of the tribe of Benjamin and that he is a Hebrew of high stature. Paul had a great image. And with respect to the law, Paul was a Pharisee, a member of a group that was highly specialized in the Mosaic Law.

These were not his only reasons to brag if he had wanted to: "as for zeal, persecuting the church; as for righteousness based on the law, faultless."

No one could match Paul's zeal, righteousness, or persecution of the church. According to the law given by Moses, he was blameless and right in the eyes of God.

Then his words get to his point. While he once thought these credentials were valuable, he now considers all of them a loss, even garbage! Why? Because of the worth of knowing Jesus, Paul had to lose everything to give his image credibility. For Paul, it is no longer his image that lives.

In order for God to get us to that place, we are going to have to go through some painful things. We can't just go to the altar and someone waves their hands over us and the image we once had disappears. God will take us through circumstances he knows we will not like. When God starts to deflate our image, he takes us through things that seem like we are losing, since the very thing we are losing is attached to our image. For example, if our image is connected to the amount of money we make, how will we adjust to losing it, and how will we see ourselves when the money deteriorates? God will remove anything that supports or uplifts our image. He will not only allow us to suffer privately, but he will also allow people to gain insight about what we are experiencing in our personal lives. Remember Job, a godly man who began to loathe his life when everything he owned was taken suddenly and his reproach of his life happened openly among peers (Job 19:1–19). Such humiliation is difficult to handle when people remember how much you had and can now see where you are.

Money, fame, social position, and other things connected to us give us an identity, and we will struggle to let go of what people once knew to be true about us. When our image is our strength, we brag. We tell people, "I am a giver," not realizing that our identity is connected to *having*. We gave, in other words, because we possessed. But what happens when we no longer have? This is the moment God is ready to get to our identity, showing us we are not who we really think we are. In fact, who we thought we were just gave people a perspective of us that is not part of our true character.

True character arises when we lose. We will not know if we are true givers until what we always had is gone. The way we react when our surplus is gone or when we encounter unexpected circumstances is really who we are. Ask yourself this: Am I still a giver when my excess is no more?

When our identity is connected to certain things, God in his wisdom will orchestrate particular situations to take place in order to touch what we have created. If we have not reached this stage of maturity with God yet, we may think he is cruel. The love of God, however, is actually touching these areas in our lives before we fail later on in our walks with him, and that is an act of love.

WHEN OUR IMAGE IS OUR IDOL

The image we have created for ourselves has a way of becoming an idol in our lives. We will begin to serve our image by doing things to get people's attention and to receive their applause. We then proclaim, "Thank God" for the image, but in our hearts, we are taking all of the praise.

What preachers fail to teach about discipleship is that when we walk with God, *we are going to lose*. You cannot teach discipleship apart from teaching the concept of losing (Luke 9:57–62). God allows us to lose so that he can test our motives for serving him. We have developed this mindset where we believe we should always win because we are walking with God. But there will be seasons and moments when we will find ourselves on the losing end of the stick. We have been told that serving Christ will ensure that we are winners. But that is not true. Yes, we may end up experiencing victory in the end, but there will be moments of loss.

When God begins the stage of disidentification, he will cause each one of us to lose. Everything will begin to go wrong in our lives. You may be the one who gets the lower-level job or the one who gets looked over for the promotion, although you are well qualified. You may be the one serving Christ, yet you have all the problems. You are worshiping and praying yet still losing. Even after fasting, you find victory is far from you.

If we are being taught everything else except the concept of losing, we are not moving toward true biblical discipleship. Rather, we are feeding more and more off of the false American version of discipleship that allows one to keep everything as he or she walks with God. But why would God change to accept this view now when he led people such as Peter to drop everything in order to follow Christ? Or what about Matthew, a tax collector making money on the backs of the people, who gave up his income to follow God? Contrary to popular belief, God's standards remain the same. You will have to forsake what has been a part of you for so long if you truly want to follow him.

WHEN LOSING HITS US HARD

*I*t does not take long for your attitude or temperament to change when you start to lose the very things that made you who you are. When you choose to serve God and everything starts to be stripped from you, his work in you can do something to your heart. Situations where you lose possessions, people, rank, status, and even your good image of yourself can turn your heart into stone. It's at this moment when God starts to work on this view of yourself that wants to look out of the wrong lens.

Some leaders teach that all we have to do is praise our way out of bad situations. Our response to this demand results in getting laryngitis—and yet we are still losing. What is the problem? Doesn't God see us out when we offer him praise? Let us make something clear: praise will not bring us out every time we find ourselves in a circumstance. Praising God through good and bad times is an indication of our faith and not a plea to be rescued from bad times.

Losing the identity God never intended for you to have will open your eyes to a lot about you. The person you showed yourself to be will no longer be recognizable. You and those who knew you will come into contact with someone totally different. In fact, you will cringe every time someone calls you gifted, blessed, or anointed because you feel deep inside that this person no longer exists. When you begin to lose this false identity, you will see, instead, a prideful person full of ego issues. You are getting to the root of who you really are. People will see nothing wrong with the image you had and will even go the extra mile to say nice things to you out of kindness to help you maintain your reputation. But the Enemy will use moments like these to get you to make moves to try and maintain the image God is confronting. God, on the other hand, is looking for you to let him break you down and walk you through this process of losing that you might learn who you really are.

The life of Job is an example of God getting to the root of a person's image. Job, who had a great image and sat at the gate giving godly counsel (Job 29:7–11), found himself in the same position as that of beggars, with boils all over his body (Job 30:1–31). Although Job walked with God, God allowed him to lose before others so that his identity would not be tied to the reputation others had given him. Like Job, you never know who you are until you start to lose. We cannot know our true character until God touches the very thing that gave us an identity. If your job has always been your issue, God will touch your job. You won't excel like you thought you would. You thought you would have accomplished more by now. Your image shows up when management pays you much less than what you are qualified for. If this suffering took place privately, it wouldn't be so bad. But God will allow those outside of your immediate circle to see what's going on within you. They will be like the people who became Job's so-called friends. They will assume that you are cursed or have an unconfessed sin that is the cause of what you are going through. Eventually, all these things will work on you mentally. So God, in his love, will speak a right word to you, at the right time, to offer you encouragement. But as you continue to hear what people are saying about you, your mind will begin to think that perhaps what they are saying is true.

Those thoughts are the Enemy's way of getting to you, and if you are not careful, the Enemy will use these thoughts to make you think that you missed God. Thus, you find yourself in a double struggle, because you not only have to deal with what you see but also what is going on within you. On one hand, you could see the circumstances and learn to adjust to them. But when what is going on inside starts to align with what you see outside, it is difficult to tell people what is going on because you really have no idea what's going on yourself. You know something is wrong, but you get frustrated trying to explain it. This is the process of God crucifying you. He is killing the *"I."* However, it's hard to crucify the flesh when we believe it still has something to offer. That is disidentification. God is getting to the image.

Paul says that the things that were gain to him, these things he counted as loss for Christ. What we thought were additions, once we got in Christ, they were actually subtractions. This is the struggle in transition. When God comes in and initiates change in our lives, he does this to get us to make a decision. The reason disidentification is so painful is because all transition begins with something ending. Transition feels like death because what was a part of us has to end. The longer something has been a part of our lives, the more it will hurt or cost us to remove it. This is the reason it was so hard for the children of Israel to come out of Egypt.

Egypt was all they had known, so God couldn't take them directly from Egypt to the Promised Land. There had to be a period of detox and deprogramming. He had to cut things off that he did not intend to be a part of their lives. Transition began when they left Egypt. Likewise, transition for us will begin as something comes to an end in our lives.

Consider marriage. It is a blessing when God sends you a spouse. However, marriage also signifies a transition because it is the ending of singleness. Every type of mindset you had in singleness has to come to an end. Your ideology—how you view things, see things, and what you deem as important—ceases. The independent mindset has to end. Everything that was "I" and "mine" is now "we" and "ours." The benefits of marriage are great, but one must understand that a transition must take place. Regardless of how great your single life may have been, something has to end. There are some things you take with you into a marriage, but then there are those things that must cease. You will find out how much you really love your spouse after the honeymoon. You will find out how much you were willing to go through to be with your husband or wife after the love-struck stage. When others criticize your marriage, you will find out just how much it will cost you to be with your beloved and whether or not it was worth it.

WHEN LOSING MAKES US QUESTION WHO WE ARE

a good definition of *disidentification* is "the end of something in your life that has made you who you are." It also means "to relinquish an identity." This is tough because not only is God calling you to cut something off, but what you lose is what gave you an identity. So, almost simultaneously you have to let go of something and lose yourself in the act. You're left wondering, "Who am I?"

The struggle in the church is because we do not want to serve God not knowing who we are. What keeps us serving God is knowing who we are in him. But God will bring us to the point where each of us will be clueless. The question then becomes, "Can I serve God not knowing who I am and continue serving him until he reveals who I am?"

You may feel like you're serving, but you still feel empty because you don't know who you are. When you don't know who you are to the point that you become desperate, you are more vulnerable to people giving you a label. This is when there is a danger of falling victim to the words of false prophets, believing who and what they say you are when God says otherwise.

The disciples had to walk for years learning who Jesus was without even knowing their own identity. Similarly, God will bring you to a place where the only things you know about yourself is that you belong to Jesus and the only good thing in you is Christ; everything else is decaying and unclear. At this moment, you must be very careful and very watchful of your cunning Enemy, who will have you looking at others who already know who they are—their identity in Christ—and wondering if God loves them more than he loves you.

Not knowing who we are during this process of disidentification is part of God's way of making sure we don't create another identity. Spiritual identity theft is running rampant in the church. We have too many people looking and talking like others who they admire. People are adapting the way of those whom they consider popular, hoping they will become popular too. We know there are laws that make it a crime to take on another person's identity. Think of how much more dangerous it is to steal someone's spiritual identity.

Christ will conceal who you are in order to keep you in this place of dependence, waiting on him until he tells you who you are in him. Once God reveals who you are, no one can ever change it. Whatever man places on you changes. The identity you create for yourself changes. All the Enemy has to do is change your circumstances to get you to question God. But God will take you through the process so that after you have served him for a while, the Enemy cannot destroy the image God has given you.

Losing the "you" is painful, especially if you're trying to live by a perceived reputation. Instead, live by the image Christ has already given you. If you don't yet know who you are in God, then live knowing that you are in his will and are, therefore, saved. Look through the lens of Scripture and see Paul who, according to Galatians chapter 1, exceeded his contemporaries. He sat at the feet of Gamaliel, a leading authority in the Sanhedrin (Acts 22:3). Yet when he came to Christ, the Lord did not want any of his training. God rejected everything he had earned and worked for that gave him an identity once Paul came to him. In Philippians 3:8, Paul says that he suffered the loss of all things that he might gain Christ. He counted his accomplishments as manure. Paul says that everything the Jewish men sought after to give them their status—all that the culture wanted—was of no worth to God.

There is a possibility that you can be working to prove your worth to society, yet God sees no value in what you have obtained or the amount of salary, education, or success you have earned. Do not misunderstand what I am saying; there is nothing wrong with being wealthy and educated, but a person's identity should not be tied to that. For example, let us look at so-called education. The church has been inundated by men and women with the title of "doctor" attached to their names, but these people are clueless as to who God is and are severely lacking on how to properly exegete his Word. Many of these people have "earned" their "degrees" via correspondence and online schools. Often these schools are nothing more than a post office box or an office suite to which people can send money to buy their credentials. These doctor titles are not legitimate awards, nor are they earned from accredited educational institutions; some people simply claim the title for themselves. Why would someone go through great lengths to do this? They plan to use degrees and titles to build their credibility so that uninitiated people will believe they know whereof they speak.

This sort of behavior is the reason Christ rebuked the spiritual leaders of Israel. Matthew 23 describes how Christ chided these leaders for their prideful displays to seek public recognition. They plan to be awarded with places of prominence, and their spiritual titles would emphasize their superiority. To be clear, Christ was not against people having titles; he was against people whose heart coveted such recognition that exalting themselves over others and demanding respect because of those titles were their ambition.

We see this clearly in one sector of today's church, where people are "racing" to become apostles. Everywhere you turn, someone is an "apostle;" this title has been used disgracefully and with deception. Many assume that Ephesians 4, Paul's list of functional gifts among leadership, is a hierarchical ladder. The spirt of pride has caused many to conclude that because Paul mentions the term *apostle* first that it must be the greatest or the most powerful. And because of this error, many have made themselves something they cannot define with biblical texts. We should not solely depend on our degrees or titles to open doors for us. It's important for us to know that it is not our ability but *him* who makes things possible. When walking with God, he will show you that it was never you—it is because of him that you have the career or business. Society says go to school, get your four-year degree, and when you graduate, you can get the job that affords you the lifestyle you have always wanted. When you are in God, you realize that those promises mean nothing if God does not open the door.

As a pastor, I'm often approached by people who have accumulated substantial amounts of debt in student loans, only to be working in careers that are different from the degrees they worked so hard for and wondering where they went wrong. It's usually a painful conversation to have, but

God is faithful. In the midst of it all, God has a way of showing them that he can open doors that even their degrees could not have qualified them for. Joseph did not have the expected qualifications to be next in command under Pharaoh. He was a Hebrew who initially knew nothing about the ways of Egypt. But, God took him through a disidentification process. If he had only known from the beginning that his life would mirror a foreshadowing of the coming Messiah's life, he would have been able to see things differently. These examples show how much Joseph's life foreshadowed the coming of Christ:

- He was beloved by his father, just as Christ was; he was sent by his father to check on the well-being of his brothers, just as Christ was sent to his own brethren.
- He was hated and envied by his brothers, just as Christ was hated and envied.
- He was betrayed by his brothers and sold into the hands of Gentiles, only to end up saving the posterity of Israel and others from famine and death. Christ was betrayed by his people and given into the hands of Gentiles, only for him to be the Savior of humankind.
- He was betrayed by Judah, who convinced the brothers to sell him for twenty shekels of silver, just as Christ was betrayed by Judas for thirty pieces of silver. (In Hebrew Judah and Judas have the same meaning, *Yehudah*.)
- He was in prison with two other men. One life was spared in three days while the other lost his life in three days, just like Christ, who was condemned

with two men—one would live in Paradise and the other died as a reviler.

- After Joseph was exalted he was given to and married a Gentile bride, just as Christ, who was exalted and became a Bridegroom to his heavenly Bride, the church.

Joseph and his brothers knew Joseph was his father's favorite. The special coat his father made him identified him as highly favored. So, it was no surprise that the first thing the brothers did when they plotted against him was strip him of his robe. God was tearing away the identity of Joseph and then sending him to Egypt where no one knew who he was. God was making sure that Joseph knew when he became second in charge, it would not be because of his robe or his favor with his father. God was going to give him favor in a strange land, a place where no one knew him or his father. Joseph had to be sold by his own family. He had to be separated from his father, who did not even know that he was living.

This entire betrayal put a hole in Joseph's heart. And still God did not stop the process to make Joseph feel better. God does not mind inconveniencing us temporarily since he knows the hardship will produce eternal fruit. Thirteen years went by before Joseph's dream was fulfilled. What if he became bitter or resentful about circumstances he endured? If he took them as personal attacks, he could not be effective in God's plan. Instead, Joseph understood he was in such a place because this is where God wanted him to be to preserve his people (Gen. 50:15–21).

EVERYTHING IS UNDER GOD'S CONTROL

*C*an you help people you know have hurt you? Can you be in a position of power and not pay them back? Just like Joseph, the disidentification process breaks your desire to pay back. The trials break you down through suffering so there is no revenge in you. If you think about it, how was Joseph ever going to get to Egypt? God had to allow his brothers to sell him. Joseph had a dream, but he did not know the location of the dream. God only revealed to him the end of the dream. God, knowing where the location was, got into his brothers' plans to help move Joseph where he needed to be.

God will use people who dislike us to get us to our predetermined destination. We have to be betrayed, and not by a stranger but by someone we know. We are conditioned to believe that betrayal is always the result of a loss. For example, a spiritual leader may feel hatred toward a person when he or she leaves the leader's church. The leader may feel the loss is a reflection of his character and may "curse" people when they leave because the loss of them damages the leader's image.

Jesus was so sure of who he was that he approached the Twelve with this question: "You do not want to leave too, do you?" Though Jesus was secure in his image, Simon Peter showed he, too, understood: "Lord, to whom shall we go? You have the words of eternal life. We have come to believe and to know that you are the Holy One of God" (John 6:65–69). Jesus understood that people did not create his image. When you understand that God is the one who gives you your image, you stop living off the applause of others.

When you cannot clearly identify what is going on in your life, the process can be God removing your identity and crucifying "*I*." This one letter is deadly. You even find it in the middle of "sin" and in the middle of "pride." When God's desire is to snatch you from sin and a prideful way of living, he will come after your whole being. He does this by crucifying you and snatching away things you are not prepared to lose or let go. When you walk with God, he does not require you to give up stuff you are tired of. Instead, he calls you to give up the things you like and struggle to let go of.

Whoever told you this was going to be easy and that all you have to do is to repeat a simple prayer was not truthful. Your love will be measured when God strips your identity. All of the songs you sing to God, telling him how much you love him—A.W. Tozer has commented, "Christians don't tell lies, they just go to church and sing them." But the true test will be this: Can you still worship him when you are going through a trial that seems like it has no ending? You'll even focus on Satan, telling him, "Get behind me!" But it is not at all him. It is God.

When you discover what is happening is the Lord's doing, you might be tempted to say, "Lord, it's not fair. This is not right!" When our flesh believes that things are unfair, we have the tendency to go into self-perseveration mode to defend ourselves. *If God did not allow his Son to defend himself, why do we think he will give us permission?* Christ was reviled but did not retaliate (1 Pet. 2:20–25). Yet we think we are justified in defending ourselves when God's very own Son did not. Christ knew he was right in his ways yet he did not defend himself. He knew he had no sin, yet he would not stand against people who even spat in his face. Christ remained humble even though he had the power to change his circumstance. But we somehow believe that we are justified in doing so. As long as you struggle with the idea of losing, you will always want to defend yourself.

CONFRONTATION IN SCRIPTURE

*T*here was a Pharisee who approached Jesus at night. His name was Nicodemus, and he was a rabbi. Scripture tells us in John 3 that he appeared to Jesus, offering compliments:

> After dark one evening, he came to speak with Jesus. "Rabbi," he said, "we all know that God has sent you to teach us. Your miraculous signs are evidence that God is with you." Jesus replied, "I tell you the truth, unless you are born again, you cannot see the kingdom of God" (vv. 2–3).

How confused Nicodemus must have been! Jesus is addressing someone who has an identity. He is not only a ruler of the Jews and a Pharisee, but he is called "Teacher," an exclusive title given to him by the people because they consider him to be all wise. He comes to Jesus with a compliment, and Jesus responds by telling him he is not able to enter the kingdom of God. It is clear that Nicodemus has already recognized something genuine about Christ. So he comes to him at night, knowing it would be considered an insult to the Pharisees for a man of Nicodemus's status to address Jesus as a teacher. Nicodemus is afraid of what his peers will think. So he goes out undercover in darkness because he has a certain identity that he must keep.

> "What do you mean?" exclaimed Nicodemus. "How can an old man go back into his mother's womb and be born again?" Jesus replied, "I assure you, no one can enter the kingdom of God without being born of water and the Spirit. Humans can reproduce only human life, but the Holy Spirit gives birth to spiritual life. So don't be surprised when I say, 'You must be born again.' The wind blows wherever it wants. Just as you can hear the wind but can't tell where it comes from or where it is going, so you can't explain how people are born of the Spirit" (John 3:4–8).

Speaking with Nicodemus, Jesus is addressing the Jewish law and the Jews' extra-biblical revelation. They believed one had to earn his salvation and his title automatically gave him status with God. They also believed they could control who could be saved by God. Jesus, in return tells him, *you have to be born of the Spirit.* Christ was letting him know that you cannot control the Spirit of God. The conversation continues in verses 9 and 10:

> "How are these things possible?" Nicodemus asked. Jesus replied, "You are a respected Jewish

teacher, and yet you don't understand these things?"

At this point, we have a problem. Jesus, in essence, is asking Nicodemus, "How is it that you have an image and identity [as a teacher of God], but fail to know the basics of God's promises that were clearly presented by the prophets?"

After Nicodemus's visit to Jesus, we hear nothing else from him in John 3. Jesus was confronting someone who was spiritual but not yet a believer in Jesus as Savior. There are only two more places where we find Nicodemus appearing in Scripture. We read about Nicodemus in John 7, when there is a dispute regarding Jesus and Nicodemus tells the Pharisees to give Jesus the opportunity to defend himself. The Pharisees then inquire about his loyalty, wondering if he has become a follower of Jesus. This is the first evidence of transformation in the life of Nicodemus. He had first approached Christ at night, concerned about his reputation and identity, and is now willing to stand up for what he believes despite the cost. Nicodemus's actions are evidence that a transition has begun. John records later that Nicodemus is one of the two men who takes care of Jesus' body after he dies on the cross (John 19:39).

Christ will break down a person's image to qualify him or her to handle his body: the church. You cannot handle the Lord's body until he alters your image. The fact that Nicodemus prepares Christ's body tells us that he has understood the point Jesus was making when the two of them spoke that night. There is a transition that has happened in Nicodemus.

Why would God want us to lose our identity? Perhaps there is something down the road that he knows we are not yet qualified for. And he knows that the Enemy will use our image to hinder his body. There is nothing like God telling us who we are. This is the Creator of heaven and earth, Alpha and Omega, telling each one of us, *"This is who you are."* We want God to tell us, as he did to Jacob many years ago, that we are no longer called Jacob. Our new name is Israel. This is what happens when God calls you and gives you an identity.

This is the in-between stage. What you may be going through is painful, but walk through and stop trying to defend yourself. Quit trying to prove to people who you are. It can be even more painful when God tells you to be quiet. When you find yourself complaining, crying out that "This is not fair," God will prompt you to be still. Why? Because God is purposely ruining your image so that he can give you his.

Our old image may be the only one we ever knew. But who we are is not the end product. God will break down our independent mindset because he does not want it. He will instruct us to wait on him until he tells us to move. We must stop moving by impulses and trust him to tell us when to move. When we start to see things go wrong, our first response is to do something in an effort to stop it. But God then overrides our efforts and allows things to nosedive simply for the sake of showing us that our efforts alone profit nothing. That is painful. We expect God to show up just because of how much work we've put into a thing. He will allow it to fail to teach us how to depend on him. We are the ones who say, *"God, I am yours and belong to you,"* yet we operate independently of him.

When you begin this walk with God, he will show you that the way you used to respond to life's natural events is wrong. You can be one whom people view as a "go-getter," and God will bring you to a place where he tells you to remain still. Anything gained outside the parameters of God's will is *covetousness,* which in the biblical context is any goal or thing you pursue that God has deemed off limits for you.

Sometimes we work and work to get something and realize later that it wasn't worth all the effort put into getting it. Disidentification is when God tells us that something that has been natural to us all of our lives cannot continue if we want to move forward. Hearing this can put us in a place where we begin to feel like we're not doing our part, as if we could be doing more. But that's a trick the Enemy plays on the mind. We convince ourselves that "if we take one step, God will take two." But that is not biblical.

We must wait on God to direct our path. It takes courage for us to wait when we see things around us sinking. Everything in us tells us, "Fix it. Save it." We must remember Satan does not provoke us to do something unless he already knows it's in our power to do it. He told Jesus, "If you are the Son of God, turn these stones into bread" (Matt. 4:3). What makes that challenge a temptation is the fact that Jesus can do it. If he could not, there would be no enticement. Satan wants us to make moves independent of God that we cannot sustain. Every time we make decisions in our own strength we violate God.

The Word says, "Man shall not live on bread alone, but on every word that comes from the mouth of God" (Matt. 4:4). We have to wait until God speaks to us, and it takes courage to do that when you're hungry. Satan didn't come when Christ was full; rather, he waited until he hadn't eaten and was vulnerable. Satan was trying to get him to live off his gift rather than the Word. There will be moments when we will have to refuse the temptation of moving ahead of God and surrender to the process. It hurts more when a person sees circumstances going downhill and cannot do anything to fix them. This is when God wants us to trust him and not our ability to bring change on our own.

What we must remember is that God will never ruin our image unless he plans on telling us who it is he always intended for us to be. If God tells us who he created each of us to be without ruining our image, the two will compete. So before he shows us, he has to remove our Lot, the one who chooses things based on how they appear (Gen. 13:10–13). When that Lot leaves, he then will tell us to look up (vv. 14–18). God never wounds without the intention to restore in the end.

PART THREE

DISAPPOINTMENT

*A*s we have seen, the first two stages of transition are physically and emotionally challenging. The last two stages are solely spiritual. This is the stage I have witnessed many give up. They cannot understand God's silence and seeming lack of urgency to bring relief, so their hearts grow hard and despondent.

As for my own transition, this moment revealed how much I truly loved him and desired his will above my turmoil. The first two stages happened to bring me to this point. At this time, what I now think of as the cocoon stage—the stage in which a caterpillar transforms into a butterfly—I found myself internally wrestling and struggling between the old nature and God's new nature. I was struggling between my own ways and God's mandatory ways. I was struggling with the mandate to die to myself so a new life and identity can develop. In the words of English evangelist and author Leonard Ravenhill, "God doesn't patch us up. He remakes us."

A SPIRITUAL METAMORPHOSIS

*L*et us take a look at the process of a caterpillar becoming something that is beautiful to behold. It can teach us how God breaks us down into something he can take pleasure in. A butterfly will go through several stages of life in order to move it from a caterpillar to a butterfly. There are four stages in metamorphosis: the egg, the larva, the pupa, and then finally the adult. During the pupa stage, there is a complete change in appearance, character, and condition, where the caterpillar transforms from an immature form to an adult form. It's during this stage that the caterpillar spins itself into a cocoon (a soft or hard web-like covering that adds protection for the alteration). It is also during this stage that the caterpillar's old body will die and a new body starts to appear. Contrary to popular view, some people believe that the term *cocoon* means a period of resting or relaxing, but ask the caterpillar and it will disagree! Inside the cocoon, a very violent process begins to take place internally in order for the caterpillar to be transformed into this beautiful creature. Its body has to break down. The caterpillar will actually eat its own outer body to produce the transformation or the complete metamorphosis of the new body. This violent process is called *holometabolism*. The caterpillar will stay in this process for up to twenty-one days, and then finally the beautiful and colorful butterfly will emerge.

God has a similar process with us, and this particular stage is transformation. God calls it "being renewed" or "renewing," and it is a critical component in God's process of reforming. In the Greek, our word "renewing" is the word *anakainosis*. The word is only used twice throughout the whole New Testament. It is found in Romans 12:2 and in Titus 3:5. It means a complete change in something, achieved only by God's power that results in total renewal.

Let us take a look at the words of Romans 12:2: "Do not conform to the pattern of this world, but be transformed by the renewing of your mind. Then you will be able to test and approve what God's will is—his good, pleasing, and perfect will." In this text, Paul admonishes believers to stop allowing the world to shape and pattern their lives and their perspectives. He is challenging the church to cease from being worldly, which means having a preoccupation with self. Worldliness allows our desires, conduct, ambitions, and appetites to be fashioned by an age that is dying. A worldly person or church accepts values and views that are hostile and offensive toward God's ways in order to be accepted by the surrounding culture. Worldliness is a mindset that rejects the invisible, but is devoted to the visible; it despises the eternal, because the heart is more in love with the temporal; and it values the seen over the unseen. Paul was calling for an external change of the church in Rome's morals and points of view by demanding a radical and revolutionary internal change in their thinking and their minds. The only thing that could produce that type of change was the Word of God. The same process, being transformed into a new creature by allowing the Holy Spirit to renew your mind, applies now and always. It is only after this renewing or alteration that you, or I, can discern the will of God.

These two final stages are extremely painful and require authentic biblical spiritual guidance and counseling, and not some New Age pop-psychology "mumbo jumbo." Your journey with God has not yet begun until he baptizes you with disappointment. This is a time where God will dismantle your expectations and shatters your goals. But even though we have to endure God disappointing us, we can rest assured that he will turn around and do more than we ever expected.

When a word is spoken to you and is finally manifested, you will feel joy in your heart. But we cannot forget about the in-between, the part that will bring us the most pain. This is the moment God desires to do something through us, and choosing to jump ship beforehand will cost you (Prov. 14:12). It is easier, however, to flee than to stick around for the pressure, especially if places and people that are familiar to you are readily available to accept you with open arms. When one cannot handle the pressure God puts on them, he or she will attempt to flee the Lord's methods even after coming to an understanding of that which has been revealed to him or her. Pressing wears us out. So, we like to head back to where it's comfortable, a place our flesh feels at home.

But what happens when our desire to remain comfortable meets God's desire to chasten us? The writer in Hebrews 12:5–6 pulls from the wisdom in Proverbs 3:11–12 to question us and then remind us of what the Lord says:

And have you completely forgotten this word of encouragement that addresses you as a father addresses his son? It says, "My son, do not make light of the Lord's discipline, and do not lose heart when he rebukes you, because the Lord disciplines the one he loves, and he chastens everyone he accepts as his son."

As you endure this divine discipline, remember that God is treating you as his own children. Who ever heard of a child who is never disciplined by his or her father? "If you are not disciplined—and everyone undergoes discipline—then you are not legitimate, not true sons and daughters at all" (Heb. 12:8).

Our idea of God loving us is if he has an "anything goes" type of approach in how he deals with us. We sometimes imagine that perhaps he won't touch those deeply rooted issues in our hearts because "he knows us." The fact that God knows us all individually and in such an intimate way means he will surely chasten us if we belong to him. Scripture implies that God is not correcting the illegitimate but rather the legitimate with his rod. Think on this: Looking past the pain that chastening brings, we should be more than thankful that God steps into time to deal with us. Not to be confused with wrath or eternal judgment, "chastening" is from the Greek word *paideia*. It denotes the process of growing up a child into maturity through the means of direction, instruction, teaching, and even discipline and chastisement. This form of training takes place to touch our character, whether through a series of events, a spoken word, or even an unforeseen circumstance.

The author of Hebrews adds, "No discipline seems

pleasant at the time, but painful. Later on, however, it produces a harvest of righteousness and peace for those who have been trained by it" (12:11). Do you see what chastening brings us to? It brings us to a place where we are able to share in God's holiness. Before God allows you to enjoy any blessing he has for you, before he allows you to partake in his purpose for your life, he will challenge your very being. Just as in the military, soldiers are disciplined daily before they become perfect defenders for their country. Holding a gun and sporting green army fatigues does not qualify one as a soldier. It is the one who has been severely tested and tried, who will be awarded and considered qualified. God grows us up during tough times to qualify us to stand and remain in his will for our lives. While the flesh looks at our "now," God is concerned about our end product: "He gave you manna to eat in the wilderness, something your ancestors had never known, to humble and test you so that in the end it might go well with you" (Deut. 8:16).

HOW DISAPPOINTMENT SHOWS WHO WE ARE

*a*s we move into this next phase of transition, let us look at two persons who interacted with Jesus and how they illustrate contrasting reactions to disappointment. The first is Nicodemus, whom we discussed earlier, but there is another truth concerning his life which I believe is commendable. The second person is the rich young ruler. Nicodemus accepted the truth even though it was offensive, but the rich young ruler could not receive the truth because he was offended. As a result, he walked away from Jesus Christ (Matt. 19:16–22). While each came to Christ seeking eternal life, one walked away never receiving it. The rich young ruler walked away because of his unwillingness to sell all he had and follow Christ. In essence, his refusal to give up his wealth revealed something about himself that he was not able to see; he believed he had kept the commandments since his youth, but his lack of obedience proved otherwise. Our ability to transition will be determined by our ability to receive the truth and make the change God is requiring in order to walk with him.

When God begins to walk you through disappointment, he is actually freeing you from false beliefs and misconceptions of things you carried on within yourself. You don't know your beliefs are false until he starts to speak about them. You don't know your perception is off until God begins to show you. Disappointment occurs when God dismantles the picture you have created in your mind.

MARRIAGE FANTASIES OR MARRIAGE TRUTH?

Let's look at marriage again. When God transitions one into marriage, it signifies the end of one's singleness. While waiting for the promise of marriage to be fulfilled, we mentally formulate pictures about how we *believe* our marriage should or will be. After all, our marriage is God's doing. There are popular slogans or phrases that are made commonly throughout the church that have shaped us to believe that the man will be a "Boaz" and the wife will be a "Proverbs 31" woman. These are unrealistic expectations on both the woman and man. The woman described in Proverbs 31 rises up early and makes the money for the family. It is not a real picture of what God gifts men with in their wives. Therefore, a man cannot make the Proverbs 31 woman his expectation. We can look at some virtues of this woman, but we cannot expect our wife to be exactly like her. Likewise, a woman cannot set her expectations based on what she has read about Boaz. Boaz was a *kinsman redeemer*, a human prototype, if you like, of Jesus centuries later. God never meant for anyone other than Jesus to redeem a woman. So, there are some virtues that we can see in Boaz, but a woman should not expect her husband to be like Boaz.

Those of us who grew up in the church and were waiting to be married began to develop this illusion of what God would bring us in a spouse—that is, until reality hit, and this wakeup call still happens today. Issues arise and they are totally contrary to our expectation. Even when God puts the marriage together, we will encounter disappointment. The picture of marriage that we have been carrying for years is not what we are experiencing. Disappointment at this time can have two results—it will either cause us to press in and grow even more with our spouse, or get us to make a wrong decision and walk away. When we realize that the picture we have always carried within our minds is not a reality, we become disillusioned. And as a result, we will think that we have been tricked or are married to the wrong one.

God did not place in your mind the picture you have always had there. That was your perception of what it means to wait on God to give you this "king" or "queen." Paul reminds us that if you get married, you will have "many troubles in this life" (1 Cor. 7:28). The Greek word for trouble is *thlipsis*. It means pressure or difficulties that cause sorrow and emotional stress. When the term is used, it rarely implies to trivial matters, but painful hardships. There will come a day when you and your spouse will not agree about something. This is when disappointment hits the heart—"My spouse was not created merely to agree with me in every way," you might think. And when it hits, things will not be as you had always imagined. Your disagreement will either cause you to grow up, or if you allow him, the Enemy will get into your thinking and cause you to feel as if you have missed God. The measurement of all true spiritual growth is not your church attendance, how many Bible verses you can quote, or your length of salvation. It is your ability to maintain the standard of God in the midst of something that is contrary to what you imagine. It is the ability to maintain the salvation and the character of Christ, although you are in something that has dismantled this rosy picture you have created.

Watching a wedding movie can be exciting and fun, but one must remember the film is Hollywood and not reality. The idea of God sending you a flawless, saved, and sanctified mate puts a smile on your face every time. And while that idea is beautiful, we must remember that a test of maturity comes after you say, "I do." Your faith cannot be tested when everything is well and you are in control of the environment. The test comes when God places you in some situation that has crushed your perception.

The process of disappointment will make you grow up. You cannot pray to God to change the situation. Rather, you must face the fact that your expectations are not God's and then live with that knowledge without allowing the difficulties it brings to taint your character. He is bringing you to a place where the perceptions and beliefs that you have created within yourself will fail. God will not manifest anything to you if you already have a perception of how it will happen. It will not overwhelm you if you have already figured it out. That is why God will allow you to get to the point where he has exhausted all the avenues you thought he would take in your life. Our minds are limited, so we can only see a limited number of ways for God to accomplish something. But God desires to show us that he is *El Shaddai*, God Almighty. He will create any avenue he wants, when he wants, and how he wants. Not knowing the future keeps our element of dependency upon him to the point we recognize there is nothing that is impossible for God.

Sarah's limitations made her think that there was only a certain way that God could bring her a child. So God had to bring her to the point of disappointment, a time where what she had always believed or trusted was no longer acceptable. God altered her reality, and he will change ours too. Make no mistake about it: God is looking to crush us. He will break us down and tell us to keep walking with him. In our natural thinking, we assume the pain to mean that God does not love us. But the truth is the antithesis. God takes us through this process because he loves us. God knows that it is painful. That is why he periodically encourages us with an unction or prophetic word. And although we may not be coming out right away, he may do something great to show us that he is with us, so we must keep walking. God will allow us to go through certain painful processes and then deliver us so that we can have a revelation that he is God.

So when he brings you to the place where you realize that the picture you have always been carrying within yourself is not a reality, don't be dismayed; he is using disappointment to teach you. He is showing you the difference between truth and fiction. He will show you that there is your fantasy and there his is truth. You will experience disappointment because God is allowing you to see you. He positions you to see the illusion you have created and see how far it is from what is real. When this collision takes place, it brings great disappointment to the soul. But how do you respond when that happens? Your response is what separates you from being mature or immature. Immature people will not be able to withstand disappointment, relying on the fact that confronting reality is just too difficult for them. In reality, we will never know how much we really love God until he deeply disappoints us.

TRANSITION AND OUR EMOTIONS

The church today is in danger because many are heading in the direction of functioning like those who were part of the Laodicean church in the book of Revelation (Rev. 3:14–22). The meaning behind the Greek word *Laodicea* refers to the will and the rights of the people predominating. In other words, the people's opinions, feelings, and thoughts are ruling in the place of God. This is alarming. If we take this Greek meaning to be the mindset of the last-days church, the people are not going to fully submit to the process of transition. Why? Because their feelings and opinions will control them. So, if God places them into something that is not beneficial in their eyes, they are going to look for an avenue to get out. Wanting to escape reveals not only a dysfunctional church, but a deceived one too. Believers will not see themselves as God views them. They will say they are rich and have need of nothing, when God views them as "wretched, pitiful, poor, blind and naked" (Rev. 3:17). Their perception of themselves will totally differ from Christ's perspective as the Head of the church.

It is alarming how we allow so much of the culture to invade the church, to the point we have allowed an unredeemed culture to redefine biblical words. Allowing the world to restate Bible truth is a clear indicator that the prophecy of Paul is being fulfilled. A great falling away is taking place because people no longer want to endure sound doctrine (2 Tim. 4:3–4). Instead, believers will start to heap up teachers after themselves who are going to teach them their desires. How far away from God could we possibly get? We are supposed to be a people being led by the Spirit and not by our desires. If we are led by our desires, we will not handle transition all too well. Instead, we will jump out of the disappointing stage and continue to pursue that which will cause us to see our desire manifest. That is dangerous! And Satan is waiting on you.

VISION VERSUS REVELATION

God's wisdom is unsearchable. So what happens when it confronts what we desire? When God confronts us, he will interrupt the vision and hope we have been holding onto. We may have had our minds all made up about how something should be, or at least how it is going to be, and God then tells us, "No." He turns down every one of those ideas and perceptions we have possessed that are far from his.

Here is what he brings about: We were taught that "where there is no vision, people will perish" or "write the vision and make it plain." We have taken parts of Scripture, twisted them, and shaped them into meeting our selfish desires and goals that are far from what God desires. We have interpreted these Scriptures to mean that the vision is what we have created. Proverbs 29:18 offers this warning: "Where there is no revelation, people cast off restraint; but blessed is the one who heeds wisdom's instruction." Another word for *revelation* is "vision," which comes from the Hebrew word *chazon* and means "a redemptive word," which is always

God's revelation to us. It does not mean that everyone has to have their own vision, goals, or plans. In other words, where there is no redemptive Word from God, the people become undisciplined, they run wild, and anything goes. The verse goes on to promise that if we heed God's instruction, we will be blessed. Our response has nothing to do with a vision because God does not give us visions to do what we desire. He gives us revelation.

Visions come out of our imaginations. Revelation comes out of the heart of God. Any time God initiates a move in you, you will not have to get creative. God will tell you exactly how he wants it done. There was not one individual in the Bible who had to get creative when God initiated the task. Noah did not have to figure out how to build the ark. Moses did not have to think about how to build the tabernacle. David did not have to get creative when drafting the plans for the temple.

When God calls you to do something, you will not have to rely on your imagination and creativity to get it done. He will tell you just how to do it. He told Moses to "build according to the pattern" (Exod. 25:40). This means we have to wait on God until he reveals the pieces. It's easier to be creative than it is to wait on God. For a "vision" to come to pass, all you need are people who believe in it and in you. But plans seeming like they are coming together does not mean God stands behind them. When people's "visions" do come to pass, they like to immediately give credit to God and say, "Won't he do it," when he, in fact, never did it at all. It was all the vision and power of the people. God never called the people to build the tower of Babel in Genesis 11, but they had a vision of their own and decided to build. It does not take much to build from a vision; just find the right people who will support it and support you. Heaven will never approve plans that were created by the imagination of men.

We should not walk by vision but by revelation. A five-year plan is good in the corporate world. But in the church, a plan as such is foolish. This is not your personal life for which you have to make long-term decisions regarding your career, retirement, and pension. Being inflexible and bent on a specific plan means your heart is not submitted for God to move. I can have an idea about what I want God to do, but my heart has to be submitted to the point that I can readjust to whatever God desires. If you study the Scriptures but cannot flow with the adjustment of God, then you will miss him. Having inflexible plans is foolish. Proverbs 16:9 states, "In their hearts humans plan their course, but the Lord establishes their steps." When you start walking with God, he will not give you everything up front. Instead, he gives you each step as you go because he wants you to trust him.

We should never find ourselves mixing new-age terminology with Scripture to support our desires. It is through this action that the Enemy's cunning plans work best. Paul reminds us never to go beyond Scripture. First Corinthians 4:6–9 reads:

 Now, brothers and sisters, I have applied these things to myself and Apollos for your benefit, so that you may learn from us the meaning of the saying, "Do not go beyond what is written." Then you will not be puffed up in being a follower of one of us over against the other. For who makes you different from anyone else? What do you have that you did not receive? And if you did receive it, why do you boast as though you did not? Already you have all you want! Already you have become rich! You have begun to reign—and that without us! How I wish that you really had begun to reign so that we also might reign with you! For it seems to me that God has put us apostles on display at the end of the procession, like those condemned to die in the arena. We have been made a spectacle to the whole universe, to angels as well as to human beings."

Paul is saying he wishes we all could be as kings, but that is not what God has called us for right now. He has called us to be apostles—not first, but last. In its historical context, the Spirit of God was reminding the people of their place in the Kingdom because they were trying to appropriate God's method of blessing them from the *Millennial* reign of Christ to their current time. He said to them to not *go beyond* that which was recorded. Today's application means there will come a day when Christ will set up his kingdom and take over every entity on earth. And then we shall rule with him as kings. The church of Corinth was trying to take a future promise and make it a reality right then.

When interpreting Scripture, it is dangerous to take a future promise and make it apply to the present. That is what they were doing in Corinth, and that is what some are doing here and now. We have tried to take millennia promises about the Kingdom and make them refer to today. That is dangerous! The kingdom of God right now is not Jesus taking over every kingdom on earth; this is the erroneous doctrine of dominion theology and the outrageous "seven mountains" teaching. The kingdom of God right now is Christ ruling and reigning in the hearts of men and women. If we have the wrong interpretation of what the Kingdom is, we will create our own vision for the Kingdom. Christ ruling—and reigning —is not about taking over. Jesus says, "If it were, my servants would fight to prevent my arrest ..." (John 18:36). One of the problems the Pharisees and Israel had with Christ was rooted in a misunderstanding about his mission. Jesus had not come to restore an earthly kingdom. It was spiritual and they didn't want that at the moment. They wanted an earthly kingdom that would promote peace and prosperity so that Rome could no longer rule over them. They wanted a ruling King but overlooked the suffering Servant.

ALLOWING OUTSIDE CULTURE TO DICTATE OUR PLANS

There is a story of a man who was from China who was considered a modern-day apostle Paul. He was a Christian who oversaw one of the largest underground churches in China. He had been beaten, jailed, tortured, and stoned in an effort to break his spirit. He was finally found in hiding and transported to America where he was accompanied by other spiritual leaders. After visiting churches here, church leaders eagerly asked him, "What impresses you about the churches in America?"

He responded, "The thing that impressed me the most is the number of things Americans can get done without God!" He had a perception about God that the leaders in America did not see. Their perception came from a cultivated and cultured environment where people and resources supported their vision. So they created something themselves, thinking it was God and believing that if it was not God, it would not have come to pass. The truth is that all you need to bring something to pass are supporters behind you—ask Aaron (Exod. 32:1–35). Many churches have even jumped on the bandwagon of being recognized as a 501c3 nonprofit when presented with the opportunity. They want the government to bring them resources so they can build large facilities, develop youth centers, purchase vans for transportation, and make other grand plans. They have accepted this handout without knowing that a law would be passed stating that anyone registered under a 501c3 cannot discriminate against unbiblical sexual orientation when hiring individuals. Otherwise, the church will lose its tax-exempt status, pay a fine, and leaders can be subject to jail time. Churches accepted the status so that they could be recognized as "the fastest growing church or churches." The Bible tells us, the church, to support those who preach; it is our reasonable service to assist those who make every effort to reject what the world has to offer them, according to the apostle John (3 John 1:5–8). God never called the world to take care of his church. He called the church to take care of the church. If the world supports the church, then the world controls the church. This was never the plan of God.

In America, preachers accept money from unbelieving organizations and call that "money from God." These leaders are soliciting help, and even granting positions in the church to the heads of those in secular organizations, so they can gather outside support for the church. Keep in mind, they do this so the pastor can fulfill his vision—that's right, his vision, not God's. Can you imagine the number of saints who have given up all of their money for something God never ordained? This is no better than the children of Israel giving up their resources in order to make a golden calf, only to have it destroyed by fire (Exod. 32:1–20). When people are swindled out of their resources it is usually the leaders doing it, twisting Scriptures and pulling texts out of context to support their scheme. These leaders look for Scriptures that will keep the people bound to their agendas.

When God called David to build the temple for Solomon, David took valuable resources out of his own treasury (1 Chron. 29:1–5). Then he went to the people and asked them, "Who is willing to consecrate themselves to the Lord today?" Then the people gave "freely and wholeheartedly" (v. 9). When it was time for Moses to build the tabernacle, he told people who were willing to give God a freewill offering to do so (Exod. 35:4–5). These were the same people who had spent their resources building the golden calf. They began to give so much that Moses had to ask them to stop (Exod. 36:5–7). As believers, we must understand that if something is the will of God, he will make sure there is provision. And the provision deemed acceptable by him will not be one that comes with strings attached to alter his plan in the end.

ENCOUNTERING GOD IN SCRIPTURE

*L*ooking at the history of Paul, we have acknowledged he was the son of a Pharisee and sat at the feet of Gamaliel, the top rabbi during that time (Acts 22:1–4). According to the book of Galatians, He was more zealous than any of his contemporaries (Gal. 1:13–14). He believed zeal was a mark that God was with him and by his own admittance, he would go further than any of his peers to show his devotion. His contemporaries all knew who he was. But what could bring one having a resume as impressive as Paul's to the point where he calls himself "the worst of sinners" in 1 Timothy 1:16? He had an encounter.

On the road to Damascus, God met Paul with his grace. The three years in Arabia were the years Paul encountered the very epitome of God's sovereignty. Before Paul could preach in Jerusalem, he went to Arabia, in the desert. And there, God took him through a transition. God finally showed him that the very things he thought he was doing for God had made him an enemy of God's. He had thought persecuting the church was a good thing. There had to have been a *transition* for Paul to see that he had consented to persecutions of Jesus' followers, such as the stoning of Stephen. He was convicted to the point of believing that he was not worthy enough to be used by God because he had persecuted the church (1 Cor. 15:9). Something had to happen. That shattering revelation did not come overnight or as a result of someone telling him he was off the mark. There had to be an encounter! There had to have been a transformation! How can a man who had previously stalked and harassed Christians write thirteen letters in the New Testament? What can qualify a man like Moses, who killed another man and buried his body, to be a deliverer of God's people? It was an encounter and a transformation.

Anyone whom God uses has to be broken down. Moses, having been raised by Pharaoh's daughter, was next in line to reign in Egypt. Moses knew that he was a deliverer (Acts 7:25–26), but because he didn't have the character to deal with it, he moved in his own ability and handled situations in his flesh. When he saw injustice, he fought it in his own way and killed a man (Exod. 2:11–15). So God had to take him through the wilderness for forty years to deprogram, process, and transition him so that he could see how to deliver God's way. After forty years, God sent him back to where he once had power. But why did God allow Moses to be educated by Egyptians (Acts 7:22)? God knew he would need someone to write his Word down for the future of the children of Israel. The point of Moses being raised in Egypt was not so he could be next in line. It was so he could become educated on the history. God had a spiritual purpose behind his education. The Hebrews, slaves to their Egyptian conquerors, were an uneducated people. God allowed Moses to get the best education so that at the end of his forty-year exile, the Lord could use him to write what we today call "the Pentateuch," or the first five books of the Bible, and so he could deliver the children of Israel.

This is the wisdom of God. And because God's wisdom is so perfect, we do not need to know what he is doing. We must, instead, submit to the breaking process and walk through our season of disappointment. Can you imagine Moses looking forward to his day of reign? He had no idea what God had planned. And at the end of it all, you want to be able to look back and say to God, "Thank you; you hurt me good!" When is the last time you heard someone give a testimony saying, "Lord, thank you for bruising me," or "Thank you for saving me from me"? There is nothing wrong with having ambitions. But when God starts to speak, you have to be able to release your own dreams.

Before God altered my life, I was considering playing basketball in Johannesburg, South Africa. My plan was to talk to the young boys about Christ and tell them how I came to salvation. I just knew God was going to give me a testimony of how he turned me away from the "celebrity life status" to a life of salvation. I had a clear vision of how he was going to do it. After all, I was enthusiastic in my zeal and God was fulfilling my dreams. Then one day, in 1998, I heard a voice within me that was very clear and loud: "Basketball will not be the career I have for you! All your life you have played point guard for man. Now, I desire you to point my people back to me and help guard them from the Evil One."

Now that is disappointment! I'm not a person who shows outward emotions, but that day, I cried. There was a pain deep inside that I had never experienced before, up to that date. After all the years of hard work, I had finally gone against the odds and made it to what appeared to be the top. I received invitations to participate in various international basketball tryouts. I was a few months from being the first in my immediate family to graduate from college. Things seemed to be moving in the right direction, so I thought, "Surely, God is granting me my desire." When God instructed me that this particular part of my life was over, he let me have my pity party and allowed me to get it out of my system.

You see, when you have invested that kind of time and hard work, only to hear God clearly say, "No, that's not it," a vacuum of emotions can be created, and they will suck the life out of you. Disheartened and emotionally crushed at that moment, I asked God, "What is your plan for me?" And I heard a voice say, "Watchman!" I began sharing with my spiritual teacher what I had just heard, and she mentioned to me she had always wanted to tell me that basketball was coming to an end but had instead waited for God to reveal it himself. "All the times I watched you go to practice, I wanted to tell you," she said, "but I knew how much you loved it."

God has a way of bringing disappointment into your life. But when I look back on my life, I know where I am today is the reason why God made me. This is why he spared me from circumstances that could have ended my life. I am now doing what he has created me to do. Looking back over twenty-one years ago, I can see the faithfulness of God fulfilling the things he had spoken. There is nothing else I'd rather be doing now, but at that moment, I felt as if my life was over and God wasn't being fair. I've learned over the years that disappointment can either strengthen your hope or cause extreme dejection. The answer is staying focus on God's established character and not on the thing he has denied.

When God speaks, do we love him enough to determine that what he wants is the best thing for us? God's goodness is a part of his divine attributes that is hard to fathom. His goodness is the perfection of his character that he exercises toward humankind. When we have truly surrendered to his character, then we will know that his way and his will is what is best. Peter may have wanted to be a fisherman all his life. But God's plan was to make him a fisherman of men. We are not ready to walk with God if we are not ready for him to hurt our feelings. It is our feelings, not his, that are hurt because we chose the plan. We painted the picture. It's the thing people told us that we looked good doing and they applauded us as we did it.

The Bible tells us those who desire to follow after Christ must first deny themselves (Matt. 16:24). But how can you deny yourself without the process of disappointment? It is impossible. To deny myself means that there are some things that I already desire. And the reason people are so quick to reject or become offended by the concept of denying oneself is because they do not believe God will shatter their dreams. Everything is about God fulfilling your dreams these days. These people will tell you, "Be like Joseph and dream big. God will give you the desires of your heart. Just trust him. Dream big! Don't make it small. He will prosper you and make your name great. Enlarge your territory. Stretch forth. Lengthen your cords. Strengthen your stakes. Dream big for God. We serve a big God. No matter how big your dreams, God can fulfill it. Stay away from small-minded people. Find those who spark your imagination and cause you to dream."

All of that is New Age philosophy! What people fail to

realize is that Joseph did not dream a regular dream. He dreamed a revelation from God. The more you start to walk with God and have an encounter with him, the more you will find that the pictures you created, although they may seem without sin, are not the will of God. If you love him, you will make the adjustment even though it hurts. The true test of your character will be when he tells you that what you desire is not his will but actually a picture you created. Because God loves you, he will speak to you and fracture that dream so that you can see the life he created for you. You never want a dream fulfilled that you created and God has not approved. I'd rather walk through disappointment and the hurt knowing that I am what God called me to be and that I'm doing what God called me to do. My life has been difficult. It has been rough. I remember lying on the bed after learning that my dream was not the will of God and thinking to myself, "What else can I do?" The thought of being a pastor never hit my mind.

Don't ever tell God "No!" He will override whatever you thought. Thoughts such as "I'm not a good speaker" will not stop his will—ask Moses (Exod. 4:10–12). Keep in mind that I never raised my hand to preach or write, either. The things we say we will not do could be the very things God will have us to do. Being good at something does not mean that talent is our spiritual gifting. The limitations we place on ourselves cause us to be closed to the things of God. We say we want his will, but we don't believe that his will can be something beyond what we already believe he is going to do for us. When God challenges us, we don't believe it is him, thinking, this does not agree with me. As a matter of fact, many cannot hear the voice of God because they have already determined what he will say or will not say. What he says will never agree with us because his voice is not what we wanted to hear. One of the earmarks of spiritual maturity, however, is responding to the voice of God even though it's contrary to our expectations. We hear God's will and then begin to compare ourselves as a way of dismissing our own ability to do it.

The problem is that God never asked you or me to do it like anyone else. We want to do something that we are naturally good at and then ask God to sanctify it. We come up with excuses about why we can't do his will. But God told Moses not to put something off because he did not want to do it. "Whatever your will is, Lord" means, "Whatever your will is!"

WERE YOU REALLY CALLED?

We are living in a time where people are raising their hands to be preachers but they were never called by God. When you are itching to grab a microphone, God is not calling you. When God calls, there is apprehension. There is fear and trembling. You are nervous and uncomfortable. You don't want to do it but you want to obey God. When God calls you to do something, you often have to convince yourself to do it. You want to make sure that it is God calling because there is nothing in you that is sure. Everything you have is dependent upon God because you know you are functioning in an element that you should not be in.

People do not understand that when you open the Bible to preach, all of heaven is listening. Heaven is taking note, whether good or bad. And if your words are bad, you will be held accountable. That is why Paul says to Timothy, "Preach the word, in and out of season. For God will judge all men." The Greek translation means, "When you are preaching, don't worry about the people because you only have an audience of one. The judge listens to you when you begin to preach the Word." Anytime a preacher opens the Bible to teach "the Lord said," keep in mind that heaven is listening. If people understood this responsibility, they would keep false teaching out of the church. People develop a mindset and belief pattern based on what pastors say. And for this very reason, no one should rush to become a preacher. Some people pay $500 to become a pastor—impossible! Other people pay $200 to learn how to prophesy over a weekend—impossible! How can you learn over a weekend something that took John the Baptist thirty years? This is where disappointment comes in. God will start to bring disillusionment to you because heaven is not buying into the way you are living your life and tying God to it.

In Mark 10:17–22 appears an account of the rich young ruler who asks Jesus in verse 17, "Good teacher, what must I do to inherit eternal life?" (I highlighted this story from the Matthew account earlier.) Today, if we were to see a person running and falling down to their knees in the church, we would be certain that God would save them. But the dialogue continues in the following verses:

> "Why do you call me good?" Jesus answered. "No one is good—except God alone. You know the commandments: 'You shall not murder, you shall not commit adultery, you shall not steal, you shall not give false testimony, you shall not defraud, honor your father and mother.'"
>
> "Teacher," he declared, "all these I have kept since I was a boy."

The Scripture then says, "Jesus looked at him and loved him." We don't hear preachers talking about this part. We think that because he loved him that he was supposed to accept him. This is an erroneous redefinition of love in some churches. They believe that if Jesus loves a person, he should accept the person's shortcomings.

The Lord will never embrace something that will hinder our walk with him. Jesus loved the rich young ruler so much that he was not vindictive toward the man. He was not trying maliciously to hurt him. The Bible says this:

 Jesus looked at him and loved him." He said, "One thing you lack. Go, sell everything you have and give to the poor, and you will have treasure in heaven. Then come, follow me." At this the man's face fell. He went away sad, because he had great wealth."

This is disappointment! If you honor your father and have always kept the Ten Commandments, such as not having another god before God, it should not be hard to give your money to the poor. The Ten Commandments teach us how to give. So, this ruler obviously had a wrong perception within himself of what he kept. Jesus was pointing out that if you have honored all of these, you should have no problem letting your possessions go. The problem was that he had his own perception and standard about what he should give. But Jesus knew there was one thing in his heart that he loved—money. Jesus told him to take all his money and give it to the poor and follow him, and he would have treasure in heaven. The ruler's response showed just how much he was offended by God; he walked away sorrowful. We are describing a man who came running to Jesus but walked away sad. Nicodemus, as you remember, embraced disappointment, but this ruler could not handle losing the image he had created of himself.

I say this again: We are either going to be a Nicodemus or a rich young ruler. Trust me when I say that God will always ask for that one thing. *One*, in the Hebrew, does not always mean a succession of numbers. It can also means the thing that really makes you who you are. In these accounts are two men with spiritual positions, both claiming the love of God. But their responses lead them to different places. That is transition.

Will you walk away sad because God did not give you your dreams? Or do you believe that God's wisdom and goodness are perfect and therefore, he demands our desires to be in submission to him? We can all make plans concerning what it is that we want to do for God—Proverbs 16:1 says, "To humans belong the plans of the heart." But that cannot remain once he speaks. Our love for God cannot be measured until he speaks. The Bible says that God giving us the desires of our heart is contingent upon our delighting ourselves in him (Ps. 37:4). The problem is that we don't understand what the word *delight* truly means. Delighting ourselves means to bend toward something that one takes pleasure in. It means to be so caught up into something or someone, in this case God, that he moves you from your desires toward his intentions.

Jesus gives the man an option: Give up your money, follow me, and you will have treasures in heaven. He could not do it. God will bring his people to this level of disappointment because that is how he measures our love. What if God told you at this moment that what you are doing is not what he told you to do? After reading this far, you may say, "Well, I'll drop everything and follow him, of course."

But trust me—it would be quite painful to hear if this moment really occurred. And this is because it will seem as if your life is starting over. One Scripture study with Jesus and Nicodemus learned he was not a true believer. He wasn't like the church folk of today, who would not be able to handle that kind of truth. He could have been indignant. He had a reputation—the people knew him. It would be like everybody calling you anointed, then you go to church and the Lord says, "You're barely one of mine!" That's tough.

Did Nicodemus ever make the transition? He had to have given up the title of "Teacher" and endured the insults to be in a position to prepare the Savior's body for burial. Based on John 7:50, we see he must have changed because his first encounter had been at night, in the dark. His encounter before the other Pharisees, and his last encounter with Jesus' body, were both in the day. These signify a transition in his life. He did not go at night in either case. Instead, he went to Jesus in public, no longer afraid to be seen with Christ. This courage shows that he has accepted the transition in his life—he was doing what he wasn't earlier willing to do. John chapter 19 tells us that there were people who believed in Jesus but feared the Jews. They were private believers. Therefore, Nicodemus handling Jesus' body was definitely a transition.

When faced with disappointment, there is an opportunity to either grow with God or withdraw because you can't handle God hurting your feelings. When God is transitioning you and growing you up, he is going to shatter your heart. But when God hurts your feelings, he's not doing it maliciously, as when people try to hurt you. His intention is to move you into the truth about your life.

After going through the stages of disengagement, disidentification, and disappointment, we are lost. This lost moment moves us to the next and final stage of transition: disconcertment. When we are lost and don't know who we are, we are right where God desires us to be. In the next phase of transition, we will find a different perception of who God is, and we will not be operating on our own any longer.

PART FOUR

DISCONCERTMENT

*D*isconcertment may be one of those words you have not heard before. It is the sum of detachment, disidentification, and disappointment, all together. It is the stage where one's past is over and he or she is now clueless of where God is taking him or her next. These stages work together to bring us to where God desires our lives to be.

When the three stages work together, they work against the five-year and ten-year plans we have mapped out for our lives. As a leader, or even as a pastor, you may have thought your next steps should be planned out perfectly. But as believers, we are to walk by revelation, which God reveals to us step-by-step. Now, this does not mean that having a plan is a sin. But when God's sovereignty is on display in our lives, we must understand that our plans more than likely will go through a variety of changes before we reach a conclusion. God is not trying to walk us through stages filled with pain for no reason. These transitional stages are designed to move us to transformation, where God has approved us to work in his purpose.

Before we even get to this moment, there will be times where it seems like our prayers are unheard. It is during this moment we may scream out in frustration, "Where are you, God?!" The funny thing about being lost is that this is the time where God really does see us. When we feel lost spiritually, God is saying, "You are right where I want you."

Let us take a brief look at Job once again. He was, we might say, out of the loop of what was going on in his life, even though people considered him to be righteous. What Job did not know, was that God had allowed Satan to attack him (Job 1:8). After the conversation between God and Satan occurred, Job's life took what seemed to be a turn for the worse. Situations shook his household down to its foundation, but Job had to stay the course. In the end, after being confronted by God, Job's fortune would be restored and he would receive double the blessing (Job 42:10–17).

Today, we only hear about Job being blessed. People always say, "God is going to give you double for your trouble," but they don't teach you about the process. There is a process to getting double. Everyone is familiar with Job 42 but they fail to read everything between Job 1 and 41. If they did, people would not be so quick to raise their hand to receive more from God. Job even says in chapter 23:8–9:

> But if I go to the east, he is not there; if I go to
> the west, I do not find him. When he is at work
> in the north, I do not see him; when he turns to
> the south, I catch no glimpse of him."

Job once knew where to find God, but ever since his life had turned sour, God appeared nowhere to be found. This is disconcertment. Job went from good health, to scraping his boils, and from having everything, to losing it all, including his family. What if, in one day, your income and business ventures were gone? What if everything you worked for went up in flames? What happens when one day you are enjoying your family, and the next day they are gone?

When God transitions your life, you will walk through painful steps, but after faithfully enduring, you will be able to thank God for gracing you since you would have never chosen that path for yourself. In the end, you will have learned Jesus' words are true: "Man shall not live on bread alone, but on every word that comes from the mouth of God.'" (Matt. 4:4, and from Deut. 8:3, when Moses proclaims God's Word to the children of Israel). God will teach you through the whole process how to trust his Word over what you see. While you trust, he also teaches you to keep your life clean, holy, and just before him. At the end of the day, God will bring you to what his plans are for you.

THE FINAL STAGE

*Y*our life will go through many stages, and each time, you must get to a place like Job, who understood that God could be trusted in the slaying:

> But he knows the way that I take; when he has tested me, I will come forth as gold. My feet have closely followed his steps; I have kept to his way without turning aside. I have not departed from the commands of his lips; I have treasured the words of his mouth more than my daily bread" (Job 23:10–12).

Your life will turn down roads where you aren't yearning to say a thing. Assuming, or even trying, to figure out how God will bring you out causes more pain. So you remain quiet, waiting to see what will happen next.

This can become a struggle for people with control issues

who like to have everything in order. While it is natural to like structure, we must be prepared for God to allow chaos to manifest in our lives. If we must know how things are going to turn out, we will struggle unless we surrender the unsolvable to God. The last thing we want to be in any stage is someone who refuses to be helped until they understand what is going on. God never explained to Job why the worst took place in his life. But if you are entitled, you will want to tell God, "I will obey once I understand what is going on." This type of attitude will not fly with the Most High. When we reach the stage of disconcertment, we must be prepared to feel beyond vulnerable. It's an alone place for any believer because we are required to wait on God to move. But one way we know God is about to bring us out and do something great is that he will bring us to a place where we do not know what to expect after all the chaos. Therefore, it is important to be subjective and listen to him.

What if Abraham had gone back and forth with God after God spoke to him? The Lord had said to him, "Leave your native country, your relatives, and your father's family, and go to the land I will show you" (Gen 12:1). Abraham had no control. And we do not know what true faith is until God brings us to the end of disconcertment. As long as we feel like we can still control circumstances, we are not walking by faith.

WHEN THE ENEMY SHOWS UP

When we reach the stage of disconcertment, the Enemy begins to torment us because we don't know what to think or believe. But the truth is, we are not supposed to know. We are used to controlling our lives, knowing the next step and quitting because we already have another job lined up. We are secure in knowing what is coming next because we have already made the plans for each decision. As we meet God, we will recognize that if we have no clue, only he can show us. This means he will eliminate us from making a wrong decision. If we get to a place where we are lost but continue to wait on God, we can never go wrong. The problem is that when we get lost, we get anxious. Fear kicks in and moves us to make a decision quickly. Pressure wants us to make a rushed decision. But God does not rush us; it is Satan who speeds us up so we can make a decision without thinking it through. Satan wants us to deny the fact that when we are truly lost, God knows exactly where we are and where we should go. We can make Job's declaration in Job 23:10–11 our own: "But he knows where I am going. And when he tests me, I will come out as pure as gold. For I have stayed on God's paths; I have followed his ways and not turned aside."

God brings us to a place of disconcertment so he can establish the plans he already had for our lives. This is the time where we feel as if we are doing all the right things, but still, failure hits our life. We can never find God's will until we get lost. Everyone is trying to be found, but when walking with God the object is for us to lose ourselves. Once we've become lost, how we really feel about God kicks in. God will never show us his way until we lose ours. And if we are not careful, being lost will make us go back to what seems familiar. We would settle for "I tried!" This is what the Enemy wants—he wants us to jump in our flesh and go back to what we once knew.

As the children of Israel were coming out of Egypt, the

Lord knew there was still some hidden fear in them. In his wisdom, he carried out a plan so they would no longer have to look over their shoulders. God had brought his people to the Red Sea. How could they possibly cross over? God's people felt lost and hopeless with their enemy still tracking them. As the pressure worsened, the people cried out to God, who responded with these words to Moses:

 Why are you crying out to me? Tell the Israelites to move on!" Raise your staff and stretch out your hand over the sea to divide the water so that the Israelites can go through the sea on dry ground" (Exod. 14:15–16).

No one until that day would have ever seen God make a way by splitting the sea in front of them! The people were pressed between the Red Sea and their enemies, but Moses told them to stand still and see the salvation of God. God put them in a position to see that he has always been their Deliverer; therefore, they would never need to look over their shoulders.

When God calls you to lose yourself, he shows you that nothing is impossible. When God causes you to be lost, he will make a way that your natural mind would never have perceived. That is how he is glorified. You had no reference point. No one will be able to say, "It happened just like that to me." You will experience a new testimony when God, the Director of your path, makes a way for you to tell of his goodness! Not only did he open the path for the children of Israel, but his wind dried the ground for them to walk on. God had already taken care of any possible concern. Had it been muddy, they may have worried that they couldn't get across fast enough. God, in his wisdom, had already taken care of that which concerned them. When they got to the other side, they could praise and thank God for washing their whole past away. Anything that could have intimidated them or slowed them down was gone. Their enemy could no longer control them.

When walking with God, moving to a place where you don't know what he is going to do next is completely normal. But once God brings you out of this phase, he walks you over the Red Sea and into the manifestation of what he already promised you. Ask Job if his transition was worth it.

Or, you can even ask Ruth. She was willing to embrace the only true God in a place that she did not know. She went through disconcertment. Orpah had the same opportunity to choose the unknown but she went back to that which was familiar. There will come a time in our lives where what comes next is based on how we respond. Will it hurt? Yes. There will be pain and more. Keep in mind that the person we have always known is dying. God is putting a headstone on the *I* that we have each been familiar with. When Christ died, our life was forever hidden in him. We will not know who we are until we are in Christ. We will not even know the way our lives should turn until then. God gives us our identity. Therefore, our prayer should be this:

> God, transform me into the person that you want me to become. Take me through the transition so I can be the end result that you desire. I want to walk in what heaven has already planned out for me. Even though it is painful, loving you is

worth it! If I have to be lost to find you, it is worth it."

THE REALITY OF THE MATTER

God is bringing people to a fork in the road, and the right decision must be made. We have been taught that every bad thing that happens to us is because of the Devil. We have even gone to the extremes of "binding and loosing" with two extra prayer partners, and still, nothing. This is because God is in control. He is trying to bring us to a place of change. Transition will always require us to make a choice, even when we do not want to make a move. When transition shows up in each of our lives, it means we can no longer travel down the same road. This road we have been traveling for the longest must end. And the direction we choose will determine our destination. No matter what stage we are in, everything we encounter becomes a foundation in our lives. After God takes us through this period and we pass, we will have a season of rest where we can enjoy the fruits of our labor. But we must keep in mind that God will take us through this process again. We may go through cycles as such in our lives until he calls us home or until he returns.

Meanwhile, we will never get to a point where we say to ourselves, "I'm good!" After establishing churches and performing miracles for many years, Paul said, "I still have not arrived." He went on to declare his determination:

I press on to take hold of that for which Christ Jesus took hold of me. Brothers and sisters, I do not consider myself yet to have taken hold of it. But one thing I do: Forgetting what is behind and straining toward what is ahead, I press on toward the goal to win the prize for which God has called me heavenward in Christ Jesus. All of us, then, who are mature should take such a view of things" (Phil. 3:12–15).

The mature believer understands this process that God will allow us to go through, and in it there is foreseeable fruit. This believer also understands the process will repeat itself; each time around, the circumstance will be a little more difficult, but the principles will be the same.

I have not played collegiate basketball since I was twenty-two years of age; however, the fundamentals are the same. It does not matter how long it has been since you have ridden a bicycle. You may be nervous when you first get on, but what you have learned will soon kick in. You will remember the basic fundamentals. Your life may change over time, but the fundamental basics of Christianity will keep you walking once they are in you.

The problem occurs when we are going through the cycles and we do not know the basics. As a new trial looms, it may be more severe than the previous one because God allows trials according to our spirituality. God will allow trials beyond our physical strength, but he will not allow trials beyond our level of spiritual maturity. He grades us according to where we should be spiritually. Your circumstances become more intense as you grow and mature in God. God expects you to not panic but to, instead, apply the basics. This is how you grow in him.

What is the difference between swimming in five feet versus twelve feet of water? The water is deeper but the principles are the same. We do not change the techniques we use because the water is deeper. What makes it more difficult is that fear kicks in when are in twelve feet. We are more comfortable or familiar with swimming in five feet. And when God places us in twelve feet of water, we get nervous because we cannot reach the bottom, when, in fact, we simply need to do the things we did when we were in five feet. This is how your life becomes fruitful and your understanding of who God is increases. You are able to see life through the lens of Scripture. Afterwards, people will recognize the stability and substance in your life and your depth in God. We must strive to be more than a surface Christian, quoting Scriptures but having no depth to our walks. Jude 1:12 says, "they are clouds without rain." They have a refreshing appearance but when they come, there is no depth to them. Trials will give you that depth of understanding regarding who God is. But do not be deceived. You can never reach the bottom in God. You can be saved for sixty years and never come to the fullness of all the Scriptures because the truths of God run deeply. God will never be stale. God can never become normal. Job was very spiritual and intellectual, but after going through his trials, he said to God that he uttered things in his immaturity that he did not understand (Job 42:1–5). But that is because our intellect cannot handle the depths of God. As you begin to walk in God and he turns his face toward you—taking you through circumstances so you can apply wisdom—you become fruitful. Sharing truth without application is ignorance. Proclaiming the truths of God but not living by those same truths causes one's life to become futile (1 Cor. 9:26–27). He takes your life and forms it, and now you have to live out what you know. That is what produces the wisdom that comes from above (James 3:14–18).

When God brings you to a transition, whatever he ends is

never revived. There can never be a do-over or restart. That is why the history of the children of Israel is so insightful. Besides the story being for our admonition and education, it is an illustration of what God does. With the children of Israel, their past was done with. When God brought them out and transitioned them, the first thing he said to them was that their life in Egypt was over. What their ancestors knew for four hundred years had ended.

GETTING GOD-LED COUNSEL

It is important for you to know that when you have reached the stage of disconcertment, you may find yourself doing things you just should not do. When you have reached a level of being this uncomfortable, you may run to anyone and everyone for some advice that will relieve your pain. Consider these words in Psalm 1:1–3:

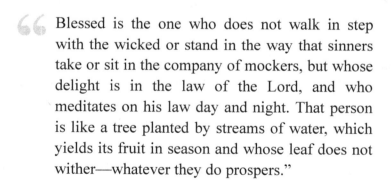

Blessed is the one who does not walk in step with the wicked or stand in the way that sinners take or sit in the company of mockers, but whose delight is in the law of the Lord, and who meditates on his law day and night. That person is like a tree planted by streams of water, which yields its fruit in season and whose leaf does not wither—whatever they do prospers."

In this Scripture, the ungodly are individuals who believe they are believers but their lives are wicked. They know some Bible verses but their lives do not line up with what they confess. We like to say, "The Lord does not mind," or "It's not that serious," or "He understands." We also profess that "He knows that I am a good person," or "Nobody is perfect," or "We all make mistakes." Yes, it is true: no one is flawless. But to apply this counsel when God is slaying us in order to ease the pain is ungodly. When God takes us, he moves us to becoming sanctified. There was only one flawless man who ever walked this earth and that man was Jesus Christ. As long as we are in this fleshly body, the body will fight against God. That is what the body does since the fall of humanity. And when the flesh fights God, Satan joins along, working to fight against the Holy Spirit in order to move us contrary to the will of God (Gal. 5:17). There is a constant subduing that must take place. If God is crucifying us, and we understand that the only way to win this battle is to subject our flesh to the Spirit, why are we receiving counsel from people who don't have the Spirit? They cannot help us. Our flesh will look for comfort when our inner man is crying for help. But God will put us in a place where the only one who can answer us is him.

God allows this to happen to drive us to his Word and his ways. Our only source of comfort, strength, or peace of mind is the Word of God, not eating comfort food all day long and then going to sleep (Ps. 119:28). It is time to load our hearts with the Word. The answer we are looking for is right in front of us. We just need the strength to open it. But when God is reforming the person we have created, the last thing we want to do is run to the Word. What we want is a quick fix from people who cannot fully recognize what God is doing in our lives. Even those who are godly will be limited, at times, concerning what God is doing. Some can encourage us for a moment, but the next day, we are back to feeling depressed. What is happening is God is driving us back to his character! And the Enemy will use everything he can to cause you to doubt or question God's character. We will find ourselves simply "existing" while God is dismantling our identity because we have no answers for what is going on in our lives. We continue to come to church, hoping God will rescue us from the dilemma, but the message for the day seems like it has nothing to do with our unique situation. So we find ourselves daydreaming while the Word is going forth. Now we begin to feel like coming to church was a waste. We are looking for something quick when God is trying to teach us what it means to wait on him.

On this journey, there are some things we can only learn about God by waiting. David understood this truth while surviving his wilderness experience. He had to wait over twenty years before he saw the ultimate fulfillment of the promise revealed to him:

 Show me your ways, Lord, teach me your paths. Guide me in your truth and teach me, for you are God my Savior, and my hope is in you all day long" (Ps. 25:4–5).

May integrity and uprightness protect me, because my hope, Lord, is you" (Ps. 25:21).

I would have lost heart, unless I had believed that I would see the goodness of the Lord In the land of the living. Wait on the Lord; be of good courage, And He shall strengthen your heart; wait, I say, on the Lord!" (Ps. 27:13–14).

Commit your way to the Lord; trust in him and he will do this: He will make your righteous reward shine like the dawn, your vindication like the noonday sun. Be still before the Lord and wait patiently for him; do not fret when people succeed in their ways, when they carry out their wicked schemes. Refrain from anger and turn from wrath; do not fret—it leads only to evil. For those who are evil will be destroyed, but those who hope in the Lord will inherit the land" (Ps. 37:5–9).

God will use the process of transition to push us toward conformity with his Son. After all this time, we are finding out that the person we have come to trust and depend on no longer exists. We will discover that this particular person is not even real; it's simply a cardboard figure that we have created. It is someone who has learned how to manage life's circumstances. When life took advantage of us, we lived behind this identity that God is now slaying.

Once you are left out in the open, God will move you from independence to interdependence—and you must admit you need help. Life taught you to handle issues by yourself. But God will deal with your pride and will position you to receive godly counsel from those whom he has approved. This cry for help happens once we accept the fact that what was part of our lives for so long is now gone. Satan will arrive and make you feel as if God is doing this because he hates you, when in reality he is pushing you into his will for your life.

What we endure will never be greater than God's promises for us. And this is why we should never think it strange when Satan tries to remind us of our past or even tries to bring back people from our past—these are indicators that victory is closer than we think. Do not allow the darkness and isolation to turn you off. If you are a believer, you must follow the steps of Christ from baptism to crucifixion, from crucifixion to resurrection. Before Christ was resurrected, even he experienced a moment where God was nowhere to be found. But three days later, God's will for his life, and for humanity, came to pass. It will for you too.

PART FIVE

TRANSFORMATION

*L*ike us, if Job only knew what God's desired end was for him, he would have not complained or wished to give up. Yet, it is so easy to complain, be frustrated, and question God's goodness when we feel like he is allowing our world to be turned upside down. We do not question God's goodness in victory, but we doubt his wisdom when we are in pain or in an unfavorable circumstance. Paul described this condition in his second letters to the Corinthians: "We are hard pressed on every side, but not crushed; perplexed, but not in despair; persecuted, but not abandoned; struck down, but not destroyed" (2 Cor. 4:8–9). Surviving God's training course in the wilderness is not for the faint at heart or for those who are superficial in their faith. The challenges are great, but they produce things in us what no other situation can. The Promised Land is indeed promising, but there will be a period of intermission before we possess it. That brief pause is called "the desert." It is a place:

- where we will feel lonely, but we are not alone;

- where we will feel hopeless, but there is still hope;
- where God will seem distant, but yet, he is near;
- where we will believe our lives are being ruined, but our lives are actually being made.

How many people will pay a fee to take pictures with butterflies but will disregard a caterpillar? People will admire your end but shun and ridicule your transformation. It will take a process filled with pain and discouragement to bring you to that end. James reminds us of Job's suffering and his ending to encourage us who will suffer:

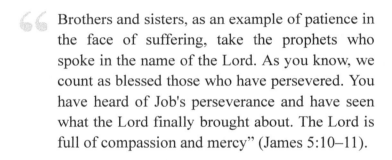 Brothers and sisters, as an example of patience in the face of suffering, take the prophets who spoke in the name of the Lord. As you know, we count as blessed those who have persevered. You have heard of Job's perseverance and have seen what the Lord finally brought about. The Lord is full of compassion and mercy" (James 5:10–11).

James is cheering on the believer through his or her affliction and distress. He tells us in order to finish to the end we have to exercise patience. On the road to being reformed, we have to endure the wrongdoing of others. We have to guard our hearts from becoming offended with Christ; we must display patience to ensure victory. One truth that we must come to understand is that patience is not simply waiting on God (Ps. 40:1). It deals with having the right temperament while waiting. As humans, we count how long we have been in a circumstance, but God measures our attitude in the circumstance. It's having the right attitude, which produces the correct output that God takes pleasure in. We must display character that cannot be swerved from our conformity to Christ and our loyalty to our faith even under extreme pressure. Notice that James says, "... we count as blessed those who have persevered," sometimes translated as "endured." The blessing is not just in the process as a whole; it is only for those who endure. The Greek word for endure is *hypomenō*. It means to remain under misfortunes and trials without receding or fleeing, to have fortitude to stand one's ground, or to survive. It means to bear up under pressure without resisting, but with an expected hope. As the caterpillar remains in a fixed position during the violent process of metamorphosis, so do we need to remain fixed while enduring our cocoon. In our death process, it's not about what we can't see or what we don't understand. Instead, it's all about trusting the One who deserves our trust.

Finally, notice how James says, "... [you] have seen what the Lord finally brought about." This is what God's ultimate plan was. God's plan was to promote Job and change his view and understanding of who God is in order to walk in the new place. God intended for Job to have a new spiritual walk and a new life, and he used the transition method to qualify him.

You might find yourself in a season of reform. If so, you are not alone; you are in company of powerful men and women who have been in that same place. Readjust your focus and finish this course, which has in it God's purpose for you. Learn to respond more like Christ, "fixing our eyes on Jesus, the pioneer and perfecter of faith. For the joy set before him he endured the cross, scorning its shame, and sat down at the right hand of the throne of God" (Heb. 12:2). "Fixing our eyes" is another way to express the word "looking," which in this verse's context means to look away from all else and to look steadfastly and intently toward a distant object. The idea is to direct one's attention without distraction and to turn one's mind toward a certain thing. Both "fixing our eyes" and "looking" are participial verb forms, which suggest an action done habitually, and not just once.

This is how we move to our new place in Christ. Keep pressing forward. There is a resurrection ahead. Remember, what qualifies you to live in the resurrection is measured in how you die during the crucifixion. Crucifixion determines submission, while resurrection produces power. Mark this down: if God is leading you into a crucifixion, it's because he also sees a resurrection. When he changes the heart, it will produce an outward change. Later, you will thank God for orchestrating this marvelous transition.

ABOUT THE AUTHOR

Tavares D. Robinson is the founder and senior pastor of Sound the Trumpet Ministries of Miami, in Miami, Florida, where he has served for fifteen years. He also currently serves as the founder of Watchman Publishing. The Lord has graced Robinson with a bold prophetic voice that turns the hearts of people back to God. He is the author of three previous books: *Shepherds, Hirelings and Dictators: How to Recognize the Difference*, *The Utopia of a Strange Love: When the Love of God is Mishandled*, and *Warnings from the Garden: Uncovering the Wiles of Deception*. While each of Robinson's books has its own specific teaching and prophecy focus, they all provide believers with the tools necessary for identifying truth and discerning authentic leadership from spiritually unhealthy leadership. Robinson currently lives with his family in South Florida.

ALSO BY TAVARES D. ROBINSON

Shepherds, Hirelings, and Dictators: How to Recognize the Difference

ISBN 978-1936076277

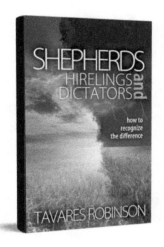

Throughout generations, false prophets and insincere teachers have pretended to have the best interests of God's people in mind. They claim they are human instruments who have received direct words from the Lord through the Holy Spirit. But in the final analysis, they do not represent God, and they harm the sheep. In this book, Pastor Robinson shows readers how to come out of false teaching into God's marvelous light, where there is healing and restoration.

"...definitely an eye-opener and a tool from God to guard the people of God from deception and error."

The Utopia of a Strange Love: When the Love of God Is Mishandled

They are ubiquitous these days—eloquent, charismatic preachers, speakers, teachers, and evangelists who skillfully argue that the essential message of Christianity is love. But there are other fundamentals of being a follower of Christ that the popular preachers often ignore. The lack of teaching on it is not just misleading but dangerous. In this book, Pastor Robinson identifies, explores, and discusses the problem, and challenges readers to get back to the basics in order to recover the true historical meaning of God's love.

"...will take you back to a biblical love of God that is discerning, dividing truth from the lie, where the love of God pushes you out of the realms of comfortable man-made concepts..."

Warnings from the Garden: Uncovering the Wiles of Deception

ISBN 978-1732513426

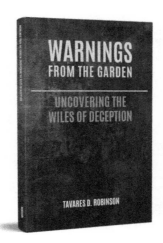

The problem of deception and bowing to the culture goes all the way back to the Garden of Eden, where Adam and Eve became the Serpent's first victims. They began to see circumstances, themselves, and life in general from Satan's point of view, and God's authority was no longer the centerpiece of their lives. This book addresses the many landmines our Adversary has planted among us. It will also help readers uncover errors and recover a passion for historical biblical truths, producing a true conformity to Christ.

"A must read if you yearn for a bold voice on this topic in the midst of theologically censored, commercialized, seeker-friendly fluff."

CPSIA information can be obtained
at www.ICGtesting.com
Printed in the USA
FFHW022229181019
55658672-61487FF